Allison Rose Clark grew up on the South Coast of New South Wales, Australia. As life churned and twisted around her, Allison fought back with pen and paper. Today, she has strung those words into solid inspiration for anyone, and everyone, who's seeking it.

I dedicate this book to everyone who has ever looked in the mirror and hated the person looking back.

Allison Rose Clark

I DON'T HATE ME ANY MORE

AUSTIN MACAULEY PUBLISHERS™

LONDON • CAMBRIDGE • NEW YORK • SHARJAH

A CIP catalogue record for this title is available from the British Library.

ISBN 9781786937445 (Paperback)
ISBN 9781786937452 (E-Book)

www.austinmacauley.com

First Published (2018)
Austin Macauley Publishers Ltd.
25 Canada Square
Canary Wharf
London
E14 5LQ

Acknowledgements

First of all, and above all, I want to thank God. Without Him I would surely be dead. I would not have had the courage or the strength to endure anything that has happened to me. He has given me grace where I don't deserve any and He has saved me from my own stupid mistakes. He has kept my head above water.

Next, I want to thank my children. I love you all more than words could ever effectively express. If it weren't for you and God, life would have had no meaning.

To my parents, thank you for your support, generosity, and patience. I realise I probably put you through a lot of heartache watching me make big mistakes over the years. I don't know where I would be if I didn't have you as close by as you have been. I love you from the bottom of my heart.

To my first sister, thank you for pretty much being my twin. We are connected at the soul. Thank you also for putting into motion my dream of becoming an author. I love you for eternity.

To my youngest sister, thank you for being a ray of sunshine. You're a whole lot of fun to be around. Without your bubbly and happy personality life would be boring. I love you forever.

Thank you to Andrew Jobling. If you had not contacted me when you did, I would never have written this book. Thank you for your encouragement and motivation to continue with my writing when obstacles got in my way. Thank you for being my mentor. You have helped to give me a chance at something I never thought I'd ever see eventuate.

And lastly, I want to thank everyone who has ever been a part of my life, good or bad, and no matter how brief. I would never ever want to relive any of it but without any of it I wouldn't be who I am today.

Table of Contents

The Dragonfly

The meaning of a dragonfly changes culture to culture. Their most common symbolisms include renewal, positive force and the power of life in general. They can also represent the sense of self that comes with maturity. As a creature of the wind, the dragonfly frequently symbolises change. And as a dragonfly lives a short life, it must live to the fullest with the limited time life offers it – something we all could learn from.

Dragonflies are often misunderstood and wrongly feared and disliked. They are thought of as ugly and dull to look at, but they come in a variety of colours which are beautiful and amazing! I see myself in them – misunderstood and mistreated, often hated for no reason, and there is more to me than meets the eye, which makes me beautiful and amazing! I love this reflection so much that I asked my nephew to design a tattoo for me. It now is sitting proudly and beautifully on my right shoulder and is as unique as I am.

Introduction

Perception

Wings of feathers
Wings of steel
One is light
One is heavy
One gives flight
One sinks down
One is love
One is oppression
One offers freedom
One offers chains
Both are sight
Both are attitude

Written by Allison Rose Clark, 10/07/2014

'You cannot get through a single day without having an impact on the world around you. What you do makes a difference, and you have to decide what kind of difference you want to make.'

Jane Goodall

As I lay in bed trying to sleep, staring at the ceiling (or the wall, or the back of Casper's head – my imaginary partner), I often think about life – my own generally. I contemplate my whole journey, from the first day I can remember to the present day. A lot of it makes me smile. A lot of it also makes me sad. Sometimes, I wonder 'how did I get here?' and at other times I wonder, 'what the hell was I thinking?' or 'why do I always seem to get myself into these situations?' or 'how am I not dead?' What I have never said to myself is, 'how did I get to be so lucky?'

Everybody's journey in life is different. No one life is the same, even if you spend a lot of time together with one person, or multiple people. I know that there are people out there whose life journey has been tougher, scarier, more traumatic than mine, and who have been through worse situations. However, let us not disregard anyone's pain that they experience throughout their life. Everyone's encounters are different. In regards to experience and coping abilities and pain levels, nobody can tell you that your life "isn't that bad". One person's life journey cannot be compared to another's when trying to determine eligibility to the level of pain that person is experiencing, or has experienced. It's not the same as a bodily infliction such as a broken leg, where anyone looking at them can see that their pain would be great. In that instance, if the injured person didn't seem to be in much pain, we would say they had a high pain threshold. There is no difference here. I will cope with some situations better than others, and vice versa.

It's totally true that some people like to exaggerate, but when it comes to you dealing with what has happened to you, the only person who knows how bad it was for you is you. No others can judge. For instance, I know that there are starving people in Africa, and people who are homeless all over the place. But I don't live in Africa, I don't know what it is like to actually be starving, I have a roof over my head so I'm not homeless and don't know what it is like to be homeless. I can empathise, and I can feel sorry and sad for them, I can offer them money, food, blankets, or a whole multitude of other things. Even though what they are going through is probably bleaker than my woes, what I can't do is feel it or experience it for them. I only have my experiences in life to determine the depth of my hurt. However, I can use it to re-focus myself to the reality of my situation - e.g. am I overreacting? Putting things into perspective can help you to see that there are solutions, a way out, and maybe help with having a better attitude in dealing with the issue at hand. But there are some things in life which are so deeply entrenched that they are not able to be "re-focused". They need to be healed.

I have read many self-help books on improving myself. I have attended seminars, and courses, and bought quote books, but all the positive thinking in the world has not been able to put out the fire which keeps me burning in the same issues over and over again. That is my torture, my hell on earth.

When I first started to do the "positive thinking" thing back in the year 2000, I would often feel exhausted. I couldn't keep it up indefinitely. This, I have found, is normal. When you are trying to swim against the current of your normal thinking, it is hard work, and our minds, believe it or not, use a lot of energy, more than most people realise. This is why mental exhaustion can be viewed as being worse than physical exhaustion because, like depression, it is not something observable by others.

Then came the books I'd read. 'Love yourself,' they'd say. 'Think positive,' they'd declare. 'Be the person you are meant to be,' they'd announce. But what a lot of them didn't do was actually, step by step, give me a clear guide on how I was to achieve this. Now, don't get me wrong. What they do offer is not bad advice. It is not unhelpful. However, I always felt like there was more to it than just a pep-talk to myself. It always felt like I was trying to put a Band-Aid on a Band-Aid and expecting it to stick. After all, I had already spent the majority of my life trying to cover up or bury things. That's how I got here in the first place. It was obvious to me that positive thinking and affirmations on their own were not enough to achieve what it was I was looking for - freedom from abuse. There was no denying it when my third marriage – fourth abusive relationship – ended. I'd been doing this "change the way I think" for fifteen years and was still in the same place. What was I doing wrong? What was wrong with me? Did I have a sticker on my back saying, 'abuse me'? It seemed to follow me everywhere I went, and regardless of my intentions to do things differently or be different. Determination was never something I had lacking when each relationship ended. I was fired up and fed up. What I lacked was the "know how".

What I share, and talk about, are my experiences. How I see and saw things, and the lessons I have learnt, things I have discovered about myself, and hit-home-hard realities, as well as things which, when they became clear, seemed like common sense stuff which had evaded me. Within the following pages, you will read parts of my life – my pain, my traumas, my heartache, my vulnerability, my failures, my mistakes, my ups and downs. I am not, by a long shot, a counsellor or a psychologist in any way. My life makes me qualified to talk about this topic – thirty-two years of abuse to be exact. And I am only forty-one. It has taken me all that time to have an epiphany, a light bulb moment, and to figure out my why. It is my prayer, and desire, that this book will inspire people, particularly women, to change the perception of themselves, and save even just one woman from wasted years of unhappiness. I wish someone had taught me this when I was twenty.

Each segment, or chapter, is a brick in the wall. Miss one, and you will have a hole and your wall will be weak. Some segments are longer than others, but I assure you it is not a waste of your time or mine. I won't pretend and say that this has been an easy process for me. But let me remind you that nothing worthwhile ever happens in a hurry, so be patient with yourself. Give yourself time. That's the greatest gift you can give yourself when you begin this journey.

My aim is to make this as simple as it can be to understand and get your head around. I will try to avoid using big fancy words that you need to get a dictionary out for. The only requirement that you need at this point is to really want to change your life. The most long lasting changes happen when you are willing to go all the way to the beginning. Short cuts and quick fixes do not work for any avenue in life, and this is no exception.

You probably will see similarities in your own life. Can I encourage you to not just read this book, but turn it into an active journey where you take time at the end of each chapter to look at yourself. It requires you to be totally honest with yourself – something most of us think we do, but in reality most of us don't. If you don't, try to cheat, skip bits, or pretend you participated, it will not affect anyone else but yourself and no one will know except you and God. However, you will not arrive at the destination you are looking for. This book aims to assist you to "not hate you any more", thus changing your life.

Curiously, what sort of impact do you think you have on those around you presently, and how do you feel about the expression "I love myself"?

NOTES

Chapter One

Down and Out

What makes you think you are worthless?

Sometimes

Sometimes it feels like a dream.
Sometimes I feel I dreamt it all.
Sometimes I feel it wasn't me.
Sometimes it feels so unreal.
Sometimes it feels not my life.
Sometimes I feel I was someone else.
Sometimes I want to run and hide.
Sometimes I feel I just want to die.
It's sometimes an effort to breathe.
Eating and moving seem such a chore.
Sometimes it's tiring at the thought
Of doing these things for many years.

Written by Allison Rose Clark, 22/10/2002

'There is no greater agony than bearing an untold story inside you.'

Maya Angelou

I grew up in a loving home with two sisters, my parents, a cat, and two dogs. We ventured on yearly family travels to the country, out in the middle of nowhere somewhere in west New South Wales. We had happy family gatherings, fun birthdays, and heart-warming melt-the-soul weddings and other occasions.

In 1981 my trust in men was destroyed by my cousin – someone I adored and thought the world of. From that day forward all males, including my dad and other family members, were, in my mind, untrustworthy and out to hurt me. I had to be aware of their movements all the time. I'd freeze, hoping that if I was quiet enough they wouldn't notice me. Any male walking behind me in the same direction was instantly a stalker waiting to pounce. I didn't know it then, but I now know it was post-traumatic stress disorder, PTSD, and it has followed me well into my adulthood. As a child who had no control over what someone did to her, and the insecurity it created in my mind, I developed obsessive compulsive disorder, OCD. If I didn't do something and a bad thing happened, it was because I hadn't done that thing, and I had to go and do it to put things right so good things would happen. I also had impulses to do things an even number of times or I would feel unbalanced and bad things would happen. When I started to go to the club, if I was sitting in a position and my mum was winning at the pokies and I moved, and she started losing, I would shift back to the other position no matter how uncomfortable, so that she would start winning again. Obviously, I felt that I was to blame for the bad things which would happen.

All throughout school I was bullied one way or another. At the time, I thought I was just unhappy because people didn't like me. But now I can see that I was anxious and depressed. My self-esteem received a bashing from 1981 until 1991. Everyone from ex-friends, current (at the time) friends, people who didn't know me and those who did, had a hand in my bullying, the worst being betrayal from a couple of my so-called "friends". Not just once, but many times. So, now not only was my trust in males damaged, but also my trust in friends, equalling to people in general. Unknowingly, my depression increased.

In 1991 I met and fell in love with a man three and a half years my senior. This relationship was to turn into a nightmare, one that would see my very life on the line. Think of a type of abuse, and this man dished it on me. Fear gripped me in his presence. Threats were daily that he would kill me in my sleep and so I would deliberately stay awake until I knew he was asleep before I would allow myself the luxury of relaxing to do the same. Sometimes this would be four a.m. Numerous times he strangled me and put a pillow over my head. He did this, plus lots more, for four years.

In May 2000 I was diagnosed with major depression and placed on medication. After this my father-in-law passed away, and three months after that my first marriage broke down. Our children were only two when all this happened, too young to remember us being together but thankfully also too young to remember the abuse. Things weren't pretty. There were fights with the husband, mother-in-law, and one of the brothers-in-law, two court hearings, an AVO application against the mother-in-law, road rage from the brother-in-law, a whole bunch of lies, betrayal of a lawyer who was meant to be helping me, a loss of a multitude of friends, and my sanity went for a stroll somewhere sunny. I cried a lot and dreamt nearly every night of different ways to kill myself. Dying took priority in my mind. I hated life. I wished I was dead. I begged God, and petitioned Him daily, sometimes multiple times during the day, for Him to let me die. All I wanted was to stop feeling this way. Desperation gripped me. My mind played tug-of-war with the notion of suicide and not wanting to die at my own hands. I wanted to die, but I didn't want to live either. Why wouldn't God let me wake up dead?

Between 2005 and 2011 two more abusive marriages of varying degrees, another child, deeper depression with increased medication, severe anxiety, more suicidal dreams and a billion times of coming close to carrying out these dreams, followed me consistently and faithfully. My life was a broken record. I hated living, myself, and everything. All things were a chore and an effort, including breathing. Thinking drained me. Being positive was exhausting. I was feeling very down and out. I could not see my life improving. I felt cursed. I couldn't understand why God would allow these things to happen to me.

Depression has plagued me for the past fourteen years, and I could tell you a thousand stories to go with them. Medication has never really worked. Anger manifested tri-fold for what any one situation called for. I was moody. I never had a happy medium and was nearly always on edge, expecting something to always go wrong. Suicidal thoughts remained a close knit friend who would drop in periodically, especially during extremely stressful situations or if my emotions were overwhelming. It seemed to always be the instant solution for everything. Since the end of 2001, the only reason why I haven't followed through with any of my suicidal desires, though intense, was the thought of not seeing my kids and them having to deal with not having their mum around – and all the questions they'd have as to why. That means that staying alive has been a fierce battle against the mind constantly, and daily.

At the beginning of 2014 I attended the Black Dog Institute in a bid to find out what was wrong with me. I was feeling like I was losing my mind in my third marriage, and my psychologist felt there was more to this "depression" than depression. They diagnosed me with bipolar type 2, PTSD, OCD, and panic disorder. My psychiatrist has identified borderline personality disorder as well. During my third marriage I struggled big time with suicidal tendencies. Each marriage has seen my suicidal intensities increase tenfold. As my third marriage came to an end, my whole being –

heart, mind, body and soul – was mentally, physically, and emotionally tired. Totally and utterly exhausted! I could not walk another step. My outward exterior lied because on the inside I had collapsed into a million little pieces. For me, I had finally reached the ultimate down and out. I could not go back. There was no future there, only death.

Throughout my whole life I have hated myself, thought I was worth nothing and that life was not worth living because nothing but bad things ever happened to me. I did not like the person in the mirror. In fact, most of the time I couldn't even look at her. That person was ugly. Nobody liked her. Even her friends betrayed her. There was no one loyal to the girl in the mirror. Not even me.

For The Reader

As with all things, you have to start at the beginning. The question you need to ask yourself is, 'What is it about my life that has me believing that it, or myself, is not worth anything?'

The reason I believed I was worth nothing and life was not worth living was because of the constant abuse I had received year after year, and the repeated "you're nothing", "it's all your fault", "you're ugly", "you're no good at anything", and "no-one else would have you" said to me day in day out by not just one or two people, but by many people passing through my life over a thirty-two year period. You just read a very brief outline of what I endured.

So, with no further ado, re-read the question I just asked. Write your untold story of how you came to believe that you are worthless. Remember, total honesty with yourself is paramount to healing this area of your life. No one has to see what you write, so let it rip.

When you have completed that, you are ready for chapter two.

NOTES

Chapter Two

Opposite Attraction

What are you attracting?

I Remember...

My life seems like a dream to me.
It all seems to be a blur.
Like my past never really happened,
Like I really wasn't her.
I remember all too clearly
The bad things he did to me
And all the time I wonder why
These things I chose not to see.
I believed all his promises.
I prayed hard to the Lord above,
And each time he broke one,
With it went my love.
Until one day I realised
That everything was dead.
I thought of my future with him
And I shuddered with dread.
He had changed into something
I didn't want to know.
The seed of love had long died.
It wasn't going to grow.
With aching in my soul
And hatred in my heart,
I gladly left the guy
Who'd torn my life apart.

Written by Allison Rose Clark, 1996

'Mistakes are often made when people don't apply the brakes but do allow emotions, lust and physical attraction to be their guide.'

Kemmy Nolan

Growing up I tried not to show it, but on my inside I was afraid most of the time. Scared someone was going to hurt me, timid and non-assertive. I was the perfect bully victim. I starred as the leading lady in that role from 1981 until I left school in 1991. A couple of my "best friends" are included in the group of people who bullied me. They pretended that a guy in one of their brother's baseball teams liked me. They went out of their way to ensure it looked genuine with calls from him and letters. These same "friends" used my name in crude letters and phone calls to a guy I had a crush on. He was so popular and well-liked that nearly everyone who knew him hounded me to stop and leave him alone. Just so you get a picture of how big that was, the school I attended had a thousand students and about two thirds were either friends with him or had a crush on him. Obviously, I had not an inkling of what they were raving on about and defended myself while my "friends" hid and giggled. From that, I was one day surrounded by as many as twenty people, pushing me around and threatening me if I didn't stop harassing this guy and his family. After screaming at them that I didn't know what the hell they were talking about, and what idiot uses their own name in pranks, I was never approached about it again. Honestly! And they call me blonde.

Sport at school in my day was relatively cheap, or free, to participate in. No different to anyone else, I tended to do activities my friends also wanted to do. One time we had chosen to do cardio-funk (a type of aerobics), conducted at the school by one of the teachers. As always, we would meet on the seats in the quadrangle and then walk to sport together. On a number of occasions my "friends" left me to sit there alone all recess and go to sport alone. They were either already there when I arrived, or turned up not long after I got there. I would ask them where they were and they would use some lame excuse that they went for a walk, or didn't know I was sitting there, or thought I was somewhere else, or they couldn't find me. Who needs enemies, right?

When I was in year seven there was this guy I liked, and he liked me. He asked me out and I said yes. Due to my sexual abuse history (though not aware of the link then), when it came to kissing him I freaked. He dropped me, of course, and told me it had been a joke. I guess he felt embarrassed and wanted to cover it. It was hurtful nonetheless.

In year eight there was a group of people who sat near my friends and I. They consisted of a lot of people who didn't like me, some related to each other, e.g. brother and sister. One day a couple of girls from my year who were part of my regular bullies came up to me and said, 'See that guy over there? He wants to know if you will go out with him.' I knew in my stomach it was a joke and, not wanting to be the butt of yet another one, I said no. Daily, they would approach me, trying to convince me it was fair dinkum, but I kept saying no. But a person can only take so much pestering, so after I don't remember how long, I gave in and said yes. Instantly they started laughing and ran over to their group, who all looked around at me and laughed. Like a bunch of crones, they hackled out loud how it was a joke and what made me think anyone would want to go out with me. They kept mocking and saying, 'Allison thinks he likes her, ha ha ha, what a dumb bitch, as if!' They kept up this hounding for months.

The men I chose were toxic. All treated me poorly. The first of many was when I was about fourteen. He was two years my senior. I met him through a close friend. We went out for only a few months. He worked, if memory serves me correctly, in Sydney. On the weekends he would sleep until midday. I rarely saw him. He wouldn't call when he said he would. Wouldn't come over when he said he would. When he did come over, it would only be for about half an hour and then he would be gone. Then his family announced they were moving. I asked this guy if he could come and say goodbye to me before he left and he said yes. When it came to the crunch, he didn't. So I went over there. He didn't bother coming out of his room. I said a teary goodbye to his family and they apologised for him. Then they were gone from my life.

The next was a guy I met while at the pool when I was about fifteen. I was asked if I would go out with him, and I said yes. He was very cute and had the lightest brown eyes I had ever seen. It was a short lived relationship as well. Soon he was avoiding me and not answering my calls. One day I found out he had been going to the movies, etc., with this girl in my year, and she would taunt me in class saying that he liked her and that I wasn't good enough for him. He dumped me by phone. When we were at the pool next, he had his friend approach my sister and ask her out, saying that this guy had asked the wrong sister out, that it was meant to be her, not me. She, obviously, told him that he was a jerk. It was very hurtful to hear that it was, again, a joke. Was I really so horrible and ugly? Was I nothing but a joke?

After him came the guy three and half years my senior (Fiancé 1) who would eventually try to kill me. It was January in the year I turned sixteen.

I met him at the pool in the Christmas school holidays through the friend of a friend. In my opinion he was cute and had beautiful light blue eyes like my youngest sister – same hue as the sky. He turned twenty-one at the end of January, and before school resumed we were going out. I fell in love with him, and when I was eighteen we got engaged.

At first I never noticed how he treated me. I thought he treated me well. I always went along with whatever he wanted to do. His interests became my interests, his hobbies my hobbies, his friends my friends. My friends had less and less to do with me, as each time they invited me somewhere we always seemed to have plans and I couldn't go. I started noticing that when we got to our "plans", they weren't really plans at all. It was because of these "reasons" that I missed out in saying goodbye to a long-time friend who was going to Greece to live. Back then there was no internet. When someone moved, especially overseas, you never saw them again.

He controlled every aspect of my life. I couldn't go out with my friends or family, or talk to males including family and at work, and he wouldn't allow me to get my license. He had my key card and used my money to buy his hobby models, but would get annoyed or angry if I needed something like pads because I had my period. He had numerous times attempted to strangle me. When we lived in the caravan in my parents' back yard, he would put a pillow over my head and tell me that no one would hear me scream and that he would kill me in my sleep. When we lived a couple of suburbs from my parents, I found thigh high stockings (which I didn't wear) in our bedroom. I confronted him and he told me that nothing happened. Each time he tried to explain, his story would change. I had only gone to Queensland for about a week for my cousin's eighteenth birthday when that happened.

The thing which spurred me to leave for good (we had broken up many times) was when he tried to rape me because I refused to have sex with him and then he tried to strangle me. I really thought I was going to die that night. For some reason, which I can only attribute to God, he stopped and left the room. There's so much I could tell about this relationship. It was abusive in so many ways – emotionally, verbally, physically, mentally, sexually, financially, and neglectfully. It nearly cost me my life.

By this time my self-esteem had taken a thrashing. I am surprised there was anything left to even believe I could be treated better. It was during this relationship, however, that I started to lose who I was.

I went straight from that relationship into another – the next day. I met my first husband (Hubby 1) at the club, through the friend who I was living

23

with because I was too proud to go home. I thought he was cute. We started seeing each other straight away. It was in the first couple of months of this relationship that Fiancé 1 started to harass me. He would sit out the front of my friend's house waiting for me to come home from work. He would call me, write me letters and beg me to take him back. Eventually I agreed to talk to him at his parents' place. We talked in the spare room. He begged and cried and pleaded with me to take him back, that he couldn't live without me (it had only been a couple of weeks maximum). I tried to leave a number of times but he blocked me every time. I started to panic and screamed at him. Eventually he let me go and I ran out of the house as fast as I could. Fiancé 1 jumped in his car and followed me. I went through all of the alleyways and shortcuts to my friend's place to get away from him, but he knew the area too and all the shortcuts. I got to my friend's place but there was no one home. I sat out the front. Fiancé 1 turned up pretty much straight away. He offered me a lift to my parents' place. I kept saying no. But when it became obvious that I could be sitting there for a while, and with no way to contact anyone, I reluctantly agreed to get in his car. I was petrified the whole time that he wasn't going to take me to my parents' place. But he did. I ended up telling my dad briefly what was going on and of course he let me home – he would have the whole time, I was just too proud.

After that I got numerous letters from Fiancé 1 after he went to Queensland. He begged me to go up there and he had his uncle also call to try and convince me, even telling me he was in hospital and that there was plenty of childcare jobs up there. I even dreamt that he burnt my house down while I was sleeping. During a call from him, he told me he was coming down and wanted to meet me to discuss the car. 'No way,' I told him, and screamed at him, 'Do I have to put it up in big neon flashing lights on a billboard on the highway for you to get the message? LEAVE ME ALONE!' plus a few choice other words, but I didn't hear from him again. I saw fifty dollars paid to me out of the two thousand dollars he owed me. But it was a small loss to suffer in order for him to be out of my life.

During all of that I was seeing the guy from the club, who would turn out to be my first husband. I left Fiancé 1 in January 1995, got engaged to Hubby 1 in May 1995 and married in November 1996. I thought I had finally found someone who would treat me right. I didn't take serious notice of anything until we had been married for almost a year. Life was a struggle straight off the bat from our wedding day. After two miscarriages, I found out I was pregnant early in 1998, and had twins in the August. Our fights started before I was pregnant, but became worse after they were born. I pretty much did everything for the twins on my own. Only periodically would Hubby 1 help me. Post-natal depression developed. I was going to take the twins with me to visit my relatives in the country, where I wouldn't have had to do a thing because everyone said they would do it for me, but the mother-in-law made a scene and so I left them with her at her insistence. I went with my mum for a week. In that week, Hubby 1 was supposed to help his mother but he didn't. He was barely even there. By the time I got back, I was being blamed for dumping the twins on her. No support from Hubby 1. Just silence.

From there, things went downhill fast. We moved four times, including a short stint at my parents' all in a twelve month period. The twins were one by this time. Our fights increased as his absence increased. He played multiple different sports – touch football, squash, ten pin bowling (two leagues), cricket, rugby, lawn bowls, and mixed netball. He would come home intoxicated a lot and fall asleep on the lounge. When I tried to address the issue I would be yelled at and called names. I had things thrown at me and my property broken, and was accused of trying to control him and tell him he couldn't play sport. In an attempt to stand up for myself, in retaliation, I too became abusive – screaming at him, throwing the object back, threatening to break his property, calling him names, and mentioning how he neglected me and the kids. Even though I only reacted to him the majority of the time (obviously it wasn't every single time), it was counter-productive and I was no better in comparison.

One day, after the kids displayed aggression in dealing with something which appeared frustrating to them, I realised things had to change. I tried to address it, but was met with the usual hostility and denial. His father passed away around May 2000. We separated in the July, got back together in the August and separated for good in the October. We got counselling amongst all this, but he kept blaming me, refusing to take any responsibility. From the time of the split in the October, he accused a friend and the church for our problems. Years later he still insisted on not knowing why we got divorced.

Things didn't stop there. It got more aggressive and I copped it from him, his mother and one of his brothers. We ended up in court twice before the kids started school. His mother would hurl abuse and call me "bitch", "slut" and "cow" when I dropped off or picked up the kids, hence an AVO application, because the police could see that it was possible she would attack me in public if she saw me because we frequented the same shops for groceries, etc. Abuse and fights between Hubby 1 and myself continued at access changeover no matter where it was, even in a public shopping centre. The AVO was dropped because by the time we were heard by a court (after an extension), the mother-in-law had stopped her abuse. I felt horrible doing that to my kids' grandmother anyway, and so I was relieved.

During all of this, about a month after Hubby 1 and I split, I got together with a mutual friend, who became Hubby 2. This in itself caused me issues, but I can admit that it was my own fault. Impression is everything. It appeared that I had been having an affair, and Hubby 1 used it to his advantage. My real friends knew me better, and refused to believe it. Hubby 2 and I dated for almost five years before getting married in January 2005. The twins accepting Hubby 2 in our lives was rocky (understandable), but by the time we were married they loved him. I found out I was pregnant early 2006, and the youngest child arrived in the September. The twins were besotted.

Leading up to the birth, the twins and Hubby 2 started fighting. I realised it coincided with me not being able to do as much due to having pregnancy induced carpal tunnel. Hubby 2 resented having to look after the twins because he saw them as not his responsibility. He kept saying, 'Why can't the twins' dad take them?' It was also the first time I had heard Hubby 2 say he hated Hubby 1 (by that time we had been together for six years).

Things deteriorated quickly. The arguments between Hubby 2 and myself increased after the youngest was born. He struggled with looking after the kids and accepting it. He would leave me stranded with the kids every day from about five p.m. until seven p.m. even though he went to work at six a.m. and returned at four p.m., and went to bed at eight p.m. If I tried to address it then I was told by his mother and sister that he had the right to relax because he was at work all day. When I started working and he lost his job, and I wanted to do something, Hubby 2 would conveniently leave the house and be gone for a few hours. When I tried to address it, I was told by his mother and sister that he had the right to relax because he looked after the kids all the time. Really, what they were saying is that I don't have the right to relax because the kids are mine, not his (this included his own son). Hypocrisy at its best.

Hubby 2 had a medical condition, and so I gave him a lot of leeway. I approached him with how I was feeling, that I felt like I was beginning to hate him because of the constant fighting with us and the kids, which I didn't want to do, and so wanted to do something about it. I got no reaction from him, so I had no idea what he was thinking or feeling, and when I asked he said he "didn't know" or "nothing". I found it hard to understand how someone could get told all of that from their partner and not react. So that started the Mount Everest of efforts to try and fix my marriage on my own, while at the same time trying to fix me (my depression and anxiety had increased immensely), fix the kids (accusations of a lack of respect), and fix the relationship between Hubby 2 and the kids. We attended a family orientated improvement program with our church, but as Hubby 2 relied on me to remember it all and implement it all, without him having to do anything, it was too difficult to implement at home with consistency. We also attended a Relationships Australia program for couples. It was during that program that reality dawned on me – three years after operation "fix our marriage" started.

A few months prior to this program, Hubby 2's cousin got married. Leading up to it, he kept saying that if kids weren't invited then he wasn't going to go. So, when we got the invite, before I had even got home from work, Hubby 2 had bought a "decline" card and asked me to write in it. I made sure he was sure and wrote a nice message in it. Hubby 2 immediately took it to the post box. Obviously, his cousin got the declinature the next day. It caused a huge argument within the family and, true to form, I got the blame. No one would believe that Hubby 2 made the decision on his own, I had to have forced him. The aunty came to our house and confronted me. Hubby 2 just sat there in silence and said nothing. After many choice words had been exchanged, she declared I was no longer welcome at her place, and told Hubby 2 he should have the balls to stand up to me and go to his cousin's wedding. Immediately after she had left, I said to him that he had to set things straight the next day, go and tell them the truth. He said he would. The next day, when I got home from work, I asked if he had gone to his parents' place. He said yes. I asked if he told them. He said no, he didn't care, and to let them think what they wanted. I was furious. How could someone who claims to love another allow them to take the fall for something they aren't responsible for? He only cared about himself. But like a good wife I continued to stick up for him, including when his parents came over to confront us also (well, more accurately, me).

So the Relationships Australia program covered the five love languages, and the five fighting languages. When it came to the latter, we had to identify arguments we had had to do the exercise on. I waited for him to mention that particular argument, but he didn't. He claimed to have nothing to apologise for. When I mentioned it, he insisted in not having anything to apologise for in that. It was the "hit home" which declared the game was over. We separated not long after that.

After Hubby 2, I got hooked up with yet another friend. It didn't lead to marriage, but there was an intense attraction. But I was also headed down the same path, regardless of wanting to head down a different one, and making an oath to myself. Well, it turned out that he cheated on me, and skipped off to Queensland with an ex he hadn't seen in eighteen years. She just so happened to pop in out of the blue.

After him, I had a number of dates and flings with different men, all of whom were not right for me. They were unavailable on so many levels, but I still found myself attracted to them.

In November 2010 I met Hubby 3 through a friend. We dated briefly before getting engaged in February 2011, and married in the October. I was not madly in love with him, but I did love him, and I thought that this was my "breaking the cycle", so I went with it. Immediately, on our wedding night, a sickness flowed through me as I realised that I had just probably made a mistake. I pushed it out of my mind, and concentrated on the good things. By December 2011, he was talking about starting a church. The advice was to wait twelve months. He insisted he had heard from God, so being the good, supportive and trusting wife, I decided to support him even though I had reservations. So, the church was set up, and all the kids (all six of them) helped.

Why I thought Hubby 3 was the breaking of the cycle, I will never understand fully, as our problems existed before we were married. We fought all the time before and after the wedding. It was violent and aggressive. We couldn't talk about any topic without getting in an argument. It got no better with time. Not long after we were married, we had been arguing and I went to leave the house to get away for a bit. Hubby 3 grabbed me and pulled me back inside with me kicking and screaming. I'm surprised the neighbours didn't call the cops. He told me that I wasn't going anywhere. He threw me on the lounge and sat really close to me and held onto me so I couldn't get up. Another time, not long after we had moved, during an argument, I went into the kitchen and started washing up while we were still yelling at each other, most likely because it had been sitting there for three days. All of a sudden, he grabbed me, and shook me saying, 'Is this what you like? Is this how you want things to be? No wonder your exes left you!' Something in me broke that night, never to be regained.

In addition to the fighting and arguing, there was spiritual abuse, spiritual manipulation, emotional blackmail and emotional manipulation.

He was very good at making it appear to others that it was all me in an argument. He got called on it a few times by my mum and sister. Obviously, he denied it.

The church added extra strain on me. I was carrying the family financially, working full time, and pretty much running a church single-handedly. Hubby 3 did not have a job, and despite his claims otherwise, did not actively look for work. My mental health took a serious dive. Our fights and all the stress, coupled with everything over the years, finally took its toll on me. I was suicidal. I didn't want to face the reality of another failed marriage, and that I had made the wrong choice – again. I was sick of being abused and blamed for everything and life seemed to offer no assurance of it stopping. I also felt a lot of pressure to stay from many angles. I felt embarrassed as well. Eventually, I made the only move I could make, and that was to address it and make a decision. As every time we tried to talk we argued, and he wouldn't really listen or take what I was saying seriously, I put it all in writing. That way he could not ignore it, and he could re-read it if needed. I wouldn't have to repeat myself. After he came to discuss the letter with me, I chose to have a trial separation. Within two weeks, I knew I wasn't going back.

Hindsight is a great thing, and looking back I can see my errors. I jumped straight from one relationship to another, thinking that things would change if I just made wiser decisions. That is partly true, but there is more to it, it is not as easy as that. I always thought that this time it would be different. Another thing I noticed was how I wanted to be treated one way, but always seemed to get the contrary. This also seemed true for my friendships. I seemed to always be attracted to the opposite of what I was looking for, in both relationships and friendships. Each time I thought I was in love, but I wasn't. I let my emotions, and what I wanted to happen, cloud what was real. To this day, I don't believe I have ever actually been "in love".

For the Reader

In many ways, you probably could see yourself in this part of my life journey. The next step for you is to look at the relationships and friendships you have and had. Choose a writing method, e.g. computer or paper, and write about these relationships. When you have finished, what do you notice? You probably started to notice as you were writing. Do you see any patterns, and see where you made your errors? Write these discoveries down. No matter how hard, admit your part in things.

When you have completed this step, you are ready for chapter three.

NOTES

Chapter Three

Y Is a Crooked Letter

Why are you attracting what you attract?

'I love myself,
I think I'm grand.
I love to sit and hold my hand.
Someday, I think I'll marry me
And start a little family.'

Unknown

'The most powerful relationship you will ever have is the relationship with yourself.'

Steve Maraboli

'The most terrifying thing is to accept oneself completely.'

C.G. Jong

With each failed relationship I was determined not to repeat it. But each new relationship always ended up the same. Even though each relationship was not as abusive as the one preceding it, all possessed the same traits.

The definition of insanity is: if you keep on doing what you've been doing, you will keep on getting what you've been getting. It's a common place thing with people everywhere. They leave a bad relationship only to walk straight into another. So why do we keep doing that? There has to be something which contributes, right?

It wasn't until my third marriage that it dawned on me. I was sitting in our enclosed back yard entertainment area one day and, all of a sudden, out of nowhere, it hit me. It was so obvious. It's a simple concept, but evaded me my whole life.

It is called LOVING YOURSELF!

See, simple, isn't it? But it's not really. If it was, no one would be unhappy or hate themselves.

It goes hand in hand with self-esteem, only loving yourself drives self-esteem. If you have good self-esteem, you are probably loving yourself well, with maybe a few areas that need to be addressed. If you have great self-esteem, you are probably loving yourself right and handle any issues that do arise with a positive attitude, and if it does get you down, it is short lived.

As for me, I never linked loving myself with self-esteem, or thought of it as a good thing, and that it could also be linked to my abusive relationships. How did I not see it before? Loving yourself was always frowned upon. You were seen as being stuck up, thinking you were too good for, and above, everyone. It was never a positive thing. If I was seen looking at myself in the mirror in the bathroom, I was teased for it. They'd say things like, 'Look, she thinks she is pretty', 'No-one thinks you're good looking, you know', 'You shouldn't look in the mirror, it will crack', 'Are you looking in the mirror 'cause you love yourself?' or 'Ah look, she's looking at herself in the mirror.'

So, I learnt to hate myself and not to look in the mirror in public.

It is because of my self-hatred that I kept finding people who would treat me poorly or abusively. Some people abuse themselves with drugs, alcohol, gambling, sex, or a whole myriad of things in order not to have to face themselves. For others, like myself, we allow others to abuse us for us. It is a form of punishment. On some level, we hate ourselves so much that we allow people to treat us poorly. Subconsciously, we think we deserve it. When I was sexually assaulted as a young child by my cousin, I blamed myself because he asked if I wanted to play a game and I said yes. I felt responsible for what happened. That's a lie, of course, but I withdrew, developed OCD in a bid to feel in control of things, and detachment on a number of levels, including emotional and depersonalisation, and borderline personality disorder. My mind and my emotions do not work together. I can explain something with no emotional attachment to it. I can also block my thoughts. Because of this, I can come across sometimes as cold hearted and uncaring, as well as ignoring people and refusal to participate in conversations. Feeling overwhelmed and high stress triggers it.

My whole life I have needed to feel in control. No one could do things as well as me so I wouldn't let them do it, and if I did, then I would go back over it and do it again my way. I kept everything in alphabetical, numerical, and date order. Everything had its place. If it was out of order, I was out of sync, and something bad would happen, and then I blamed myself. This and other things made up the OCD.

Another thing which contributes to the sort of relationships I am attracted to is that I am a rescuer. I meet someone, they have issues, and somehow, without really thinking about it, I feel as if I can help them fix their problem(s). In reality, I can't because they need to want to. The people I have ended up with, or friends with, usually had bigger issues than I was equipped to deal with. When things started to go sour, they blamed me and I blamed them.

All of these things affected the way I felt about myself, that is, self-esteem. Hating yourself = poor self-esteem. When we hate ourselves, we hate nearly everything about ourselves. Everything we do to ourselves, and allow, is a reflection on how we feel about ourselves. We all go about the majority of our lives trying to "fix" it with "things" in order to feel better about ourselves, thinking that the "thing" will make us "happy". It is a Band-Aid, and band aids come off. Of course the "things" don't make us happy because they are not the cause of the problem. You don't get rid of weeds by cutting off the leaves – you pull them out of the ground by the roots.

The reason I jumped from one relationship straight into another was because I felt that I needed a man, or someone else, to make me happy and feel complete. When I was no longer happy it was all their fault for not keeping me happy. I also gave my whole heart too quickly and thus did not think too deeply about where I was headed. I let my emotions guide me instead of a combination of heart and mind. Obviously, this is as effective as building a house on sand. Eventually, it's going to give way and crash. Unfortunately, this is the same as trying to "fix" your happiness with something else. In this instance the "thing" just so happens to be a person. You are not going to like the end destination.

Since I was eight years old I have hated myself. These included:

- Wearing glasses
- Having severe acne
- Being short
- Having blonde hair
- The shape of my face
- My nose

- My side profile
- The deep arch in my lower spine
- My feet
- My body in general – e.g., white skin that wouldn't tan
- My life in general – everyone hated me
- That it looked like I had no hips
- Not being allowed to shave my legs
- Not having a best friend
- Looking in the mirror
- That I was not talented at anything
- That I was unlikable
- Men/boys
- Not getting pocket money/being poor
- Never having clothes that fit me because they were all hand-me-downs from people larger than me
- Not having fashionable clothing
- Having friends who betrayed me
- That I was petrified of water
- That I was petrified of dying and dreamt of being buried alive
- That I was shy
- Being asked if I was a virgin and not knowing myself

That is not a complete list, of course. But you get the picture. Loving yourself is essential, and is at the core of a happy life. Love yourself = happy ☺

"Y" might be a crooked letter, but you can straighten it so it becomes an "I".

For the Reader

Now it's your turn to look at your life. Take a few moments to consider what you think and feel about yourself and your life. When you are ready, write all the things that you believe contribute to "why" you attract who you attract. Include what you hate about yourself, what you notice in your own behaviour, personality, and attitude. If you need to, read back over the chapter as it may help jolt points for you. This step may take a while. Don't rush it. Take your time. The more honest you are with yourself, no matter how horrible, embarrassing or shameful, the more effective this step will be for you.

Once you have done that, you are ready for chapter four.

NOTES

Chapter Four

Looking Through the Looking Glass

What is it you are looking for?

I See You

I see you sitting there,
Just waiting.
Waiting for something.

I see you stare out
Into the yonder.
Thinking and looking.

Wonder fills my mind.
My heart is soft,
Dwells in compassion.

Upwards my head turns.
Clouds swirl above.
Feel the wind of change.

Drops of Heaven's love
Fall gently down.
In them, my reflection.

Written by Allison Rose Clark, 31/05/2014

'The big secret in life is that there is no big secret. Whatever your goal, you can get there if you're willing to work.'

Oprah Winfrey

Fiancé 1 was my first serious relationship. I was sixteen and in love. I dreamt of marrying him, and practised over and over signing my name with his surname. I used to keep a diary, and all through it was his name linked with words like "forever" and "my love". There were many drawn love hearts, some plain and some fancy, but all had his initials, fold out pieces of paper with his name + mine, photos and even stubs of movie tickets we saw together. Every entry included him and how much I loved him and wanted no other. I even wrote poetry about him. I had it bad. If anyone tried to tell me anything about their negative thoughts about him, I would not listen to it. 'I knew him better than them,' I would say to myself. 'They don't know him like I do.' When we got engaged when I was eighteen, my parents were not thrilled like I thought they would be. My mum went off her rocker at me and I ran from the house crying. Around this time, my sister found out she was pregnant. My mum was happy but my dad went off his nut. This is nothing against my sister, as I love her dearly, and my nephew, and she is not responsible for the actions of others, but I would often think how hypocritical it was of my mum to be happy about a teen pregnancy but not about her adult daughter getting engaged. It made me angry at my mum.

When I moved out with Fiancé 1 at nineteen, my dad told me if I went I was not welcome back. 'Fine,' I yelled at him as I walked out the door. I was determined never to go back to live with them.

When it ended, I was too proud to go to my dad. I didn't want to hear him say, 'No, I told you that you're not welcome back.' So, I lived with my friend. When I was told I couldn't live there anymore, I reluctantly and ashamedly went to my dad, told him what happened, and asked to come home. Of course he let me! When I approached him, he was in the garage cleaning his rifle for the target rifle club he was a member of. In hindsight, it probably wasn't the ideal time to mention to a dad that his daughter was being abused and stalked. Of course, he didn't use his rifle on Fiancé 1, but later he told me he wanted to. Having children of my own makes me realise that there probably isn't anything I wouldn't do for them if anyone hurt them. I don't blame my dad for feeling that way. Today, I can imagine how much restraint it would have taken to resist the urge. I love my dad.

Following the final split from Fiancé 1, I was willing to listen to what others had to say about him and what they observed. It was hard to hear though. I found myself defending my decisions a lot, and his behaviour, regardless of what I had gone through.

When I met Hubby 1, I had made an oath to myself that I would not be a doormat or stay quiet again. Part of me realised I had hidden the truth of what was happening from those who truly cared about me. I didn't have what you would call a plan on how I was going to see that come about, just a determination to not let it happen again. To me that was the plan. When Hubby 1 and I were planning our wedding, I was doing all the saving, despite promises from Hubby 1 that he would save too. I even paid for my own engagement ring. We looked at wedding cars and decided not to go with the ones we looked at because they were expensive. I had organised to use the car of my dad's good friend, a car which I had admired since I was little and had always said to him that I was going to use as my bridal car when I got married. It was in mint condition. Well, without saying anything to me, Hubby 1 and his mother went and hired the other cars, despite knowing my reasons. His mother said she would pay for it, but I was angry because now we had to save the money for it in case she couldn't pay for it on the day – more pressure on me because I was the only one saving. I was also angry because I had to cancel using a good friend's car which I adored. It felt like I was saying to him that his car wasn't good enough. Not true by long shot!

After we were married, and we started fighting, I did a pendulum swing from one side to the other – being too passive to being too assertive to the point of being abusive myself. There was no happy medium. What he did to me, I did back to him. I very rarely started anything, mostly responded to how I was being treated except for the times I was trying to bring up subjects that needed discussing. I would get so frustrated that I would lash out. I'm not perfect, and I contributed to the problems. I didn't really know how to deal with the situations effectively. All I knew was that I didn't want to be abused again, and I did everything I could think of to not let it happen again. In reality, I was the same as him, just as bad. It made no difference really that I didn't start the arguments most of the time because it came down to my own actions. I was responsible for how I responded, and I did that terribly.

What I hadn't seen in the beginning but continued to happen, was just how much Hubby 1's mum had a strangle hold on him. She was the third wheel in our marriage. She said, 'jump' and he said, 'how high?' She showed it during the organisation of our wedding with the cars and my wedding dress (she wanted me to buy it and she pay, while I insisted on hiring it so I didn't have to store it). She displayed it with the twins when I wanted to take them to the country with me. She showed it when Hubby 1's father passed away. She wanted to only babysit the twins at her place overnight. She said she didn't like staying at other's houses. That was a lie because she stayed overnight all the time babysitting for one of her son's kids fifteen minutes away, and her close friend's kids 10 minutes away. She lived only five minutes from us – a lot closer than the others. Then she showed it in convincing Hubby 1 that it was a good idea to move into the house with her. Hubby 1's allegiance was to his mother, not his wife and kids.

When I split from Hubby 1, things escalated. People would tell me all about what they thought of him, and I listened, defending myself and my decisions and him as well at times.

Hubby 2 seemed like an easy going, laid back, go with the flow type of guy. There didn't seem to be an abusive bone in his body. He always seemed happy. When he was almost in high school, he suffered a medical condition, and it left him with some limitations. Again, I was determined not to let abuse in my life anymore. Hubby 2 seemed like he was "the" one who would treat me right. I went with the flow of things. I didn't really stop to think if I was really in love with him or if it was to prove to Hubby 1 that this relationship was one for life, especially since it came about so soon after our separation. I never considered how getting married and being responsible for a family would affect Hubby 2 either.

He was OK until I got to the point in my pregnancy where I couldn't even hold a knife or drive without my hands going tingly and numb. He then had to take over what I used to do. It wasn't until then that I realised just how little he did for anyone other than himself. When he came home from work, he would fuss about organising his work stuff for the next day – which was great, by the way, then he'd go out the back or for a drive or a walk down the road. I would cook, bathe the kids, and tidy up, and then he would come home, eat, watch TV and go to bed by eight p.m. It's common for people with his medical condition to get tired early in the evening like that.

When, during my pregnancy, he had to do more than just run around after himself, he started to get angry and resentful. I heard countless times from his mum and sister, excuses for his behaviour, his moods, his anger, his absence. They also kept saying he couldn't do certain things, but I saw a lot of inconsistencies to their claims and what I experienced as his wife. They'd then tell me that I knew this about him before getting married to him. Let me say that knowing someone has a medical condition and not living with them is different to living with them intimately, married with all the expectations a wife and husband have of each other. I realised that he had been raised since the onset of his medical condition to just concentrate on himself, his needs and what he wanted to do while the rest of the family manoeuvred around him. He took that same attitude into our marriage. That is something I didn't know before.

When he had to go off that self-centred track, he absolutely refused to take on the responsibility of making a decision for himself regarding the family. He would often ask me what to cook for dinner, and then get upset because I told him to just make a decision and we'd eat it, no different to what I always did. He started getting resentful of the twins being there after school and not at their dad's place. They started arguing more and I saw their relationship deteriorate rapidly. No matter what I said, Hubby 2 always insisted it was up to the twins (eight years old at the time) to show him respect in order for them to get any from him.

After the youngest was born, things didn't improve. We kept on fighting. He kept blaming the twins for him not showing them respect including in how he spoke to them and the names he would call them. Sometimes, the name calling was also aimed at the youngest one just before we separated. He was about two by that time and the twins were ten. My depression and anxiety increased to the point that I didn't want to be there. So, nearly every Sunday night, after the youngest went to bed, I would go for long drives. I didn't want to be there, or anywhere near Hubby 2.

I started working when the youngest was almost one, and every day Hubby 2 would call about what to cook for dinner. I would tell him the same thing every day. Some nights, he had been so peeved I had not told him what to cook that I would get home and the twins had not eaten and he had not cooked anything. Also, none of the kids, including the baby, would have been bathed, only half the washing up would have been done, all the washing would be sitting on the floor in the lounge room for me to fold and put away, etc. At that time, Hubby 2 didn't have a job, and I would get home about seven p.m. due to carpooling with my sister and our central meeting point was my parents' place. I was accused of sitting around for an hour after work every day drinking coffee with my mum. I never did. It actually took an hour to get home with the arrangement we had. Her time frame for getting home was the same as mine. He didn't believe me and neither did his mother or sister.

One day, sometime after the fiasco with his cousin's wedding, Hubby 2's parents sent his sister over to look after the kids so we could go over there for a meeting. They told us that they wanted to help Hubby 2 and I reconcile our problems. The whole time we were there, I was told about what I was doing wrong and what I was doing to Hubby 2, and how he didn't know what the problem was. I tried to explain but they, mostly his mother, kept on insisting it had everything to do with whatever I was doing because Hubby 2 was such a laid back person that it was hard for them to believe that he could be anything but gentle and passive, and then reminded me that he had a medical condition and so couldn't help the things he did. Hubby 2 just sat there with his head in his hand and said absolutely nothing the whole time. His father said very little too. The meeting wasn't so much a bid to help our marriage as it was to inform me that all our problems were my fault. I left with Hubby 2 in tow. I was so angry.

Because of Hubby 2's medical condition, and no one having a recent assessment report, he agreed to attend a specialist centre and organise one with them. I wanted to know if I was expecting too much of him. The end result confirmed that I had assessed the situation correctly, but his family refused to accept the report, saying he already had one done when the medical condition happened. What they didn't realise was when the specialist centre requested his hospital records, there was no record of the assessment having ever been conducted. I believe, understandably, that they didn't want to admit that he was capable of more than they have ever given him credit for.

When I finally left Hubby 2, people, again, were happy to tell me all about what they had observed and their thoughts, and I listened. Still, I defended myself and my decisions, and Hubby 2's behaviour to some degree.

Then there is Hubby 3. I made a head decision there. All my relationships to this point had been determined on what I thought I felt for them. This one I decided not to go on emotion alone. I thought about it and decided that this was a suitable match, and that somehow this would be the breaking of a mould I had been stuck in my whole life. I convinced myself that I loved him even though I did have some reservations. I used the excuse that we were living life and didn't have rose-coloured glasses on about each other, and life is too short. His size bothered me sometimes, but I brushed it aside and constantly told myself that it didn't matter. I would look at the sizes of couples all over the place and say to myself, 'See, they don't care.' I wanted to believe it was from God. I wanted to believe it was right. But in hind-sight, I was never happy. We had good times, but we fought more than we didn't. And so, I was not happy with my life or where I was at. I wanted to be treated better, no abuse, and believed his stories and assurances from others that I would be looked after by this man. It turns out I wasn't. I had to carry him, the kids and all the financial responsibilities. I struggled, was depressed, and anxious. I panicked a lot. I wanted to kill myself at every little incident that happened. He didn't have a job and never seriously looked for one. He refused to do volunteer work because he didn't want to give free labour. Nothing looked bright. All I saw was struggle ville for the rest of my life. Everything seemed equivalent to a dark and gloomy storm – just a bleak turbulent outlook.

This last marriage is like the straw that broke the camel's back. An ant can carry many times its own body weight and size, but pile too much on, and it can't carry it. This was no different. Over the years, my load has been added to from all angles. I had reached the point where I could carry no more. I was having panic attacks all the time. I wanted to die rather than go another day in this marriage. It felt like I was going crazy. I felt trapped and confused because I didn't want a third divorce. We also ran a church, so how was that going to affect people? I felt obligated to stay. So much pressure was on me from every side that I could barely breathe.

I felt embarrassed and ashamed that I had made the choice to marry this man the way I had. It was my own fault. But I could not go another step. I could not go another day. It had to stop or I would.

When Hubby 3 and I separated, all the stories came out of the woodwork. Some made me feel even worse. I had some good friends tell me that they were there to support me, but couldn't support me if I was going to get divorced. Needless to say, those people are not a part, or major part, of my life any more. Some other good friends, though they don't necessarily agree, have tried to understand where I am coming from, and support me through whatever it is I decide to do. They care more about me than they do about my marital status and how it appears to others. That's what truly supporting someone means. Your real friends shine in times like these.

Through all of these relationships I have thought that I knew what it was I wanted. But I never found it. How can I find something if I don't know what I'm looking for? Everyone around me could see what I couldn't, even before marrying these men. They could see how they spoke to me, the way they treated me, if they were lazy or hardworking, whether they just wanted a mum rather than a wife, if they had a desire to work or bludge off me and what I earn, if they put me first or their hobby etc. This was made very clear to me every time one of my relationships ended.

The one person who always had it down pat, was always deadly and scarily accurate, was my dad. He always pinned them straight away. I have learnt to take serious heed to what my dad sees in the men I date. I also have a few friends now who I know will be blatantly truthful with me in what they see in the men I date. I trust these people with my life. But I can't rely on them alone. I have to have an action plan.

Seeing my relationships through other people's eyes was quite sobering. Hearing what others saw and the opinions they had because of it made me realise I didn't really "look" at the man I was with. I had some romantic notion in my head of it being right and he was my perfect fit – like a glove. I didn't care about the little things I noticed, brushing them aside as "it doesn't matter" or "we'll cross that bridge when we come to it". A couple of examples I have from my life are the size of Hubby 3 (it doesn't matter), and Hubby 1 being Catholic and wanting to send our kids to a Catholic school like the one he went to (we'll cross that bridge when we come to it). Trust me, the little things DO matter. If it bothers you now, it will still bother you in two years' time. Don't ignore them.

At the age of forty, I realised that I must hate myself so much that I allowed these men to treat me badly by staying with them to let them do it some more. I made excuses, gave too many chances, overlooked things. All this made me admit that I had compromised a lot, and that I really didn't know what I was looking for in regards to treatment. Many people outside the Christian belief know the saying, 'treat others how you would like to be treated' and 'love your enemy as you love yourself.' What dawned on me was that I expected others to treat me how I wanted to be treated without really treating myself in the way I wanted from them. Basically, if I hate myself and can't show me love, how can I expect to love anyone else or them love me? I abuse me, so the only ones who get close to me abuse me.

When I met Hubby 3, I had a short list but I didn't stick to it. My list looked like this:

- He has to be Christian for more than five years
- He has to be attending a church
- He has to have a job
- He has to have his own kids, or is willing to not have any
- Age does not matter

That was pretty much it. Looking at that list, I can see that it was not about what I was looking for in treatment. They are just surface stuff, not anything deep. There's nothing which outlines to me my expectations of treatment.

So, how did I want to be treated?

I want to be treated non-abusively. I want to stop hating myself. I want to matter. I want to be looked after.

Ok, that's good, but it's not really descriptive of what that is. What does all of that look like to me? I'm going to need a new list entirely. My original list tells me nothing, and the next ones are blanket statements. A good place to start is to consider what I don't want. We have grown up in a negative world. It's easier to find them. So, for me, it looks like this:

- I don't want to be hit
- I don't want to be yelled and screamed at
- I don't want to be called names
- I don't want to be controlled
- I don't want to be put down
- I don't want to be blamed for everything
- I don't want to be the only breadwinner
- I don't want someone lazy
- I don't want someone who is an "ima gonna"
- I don't want to come second

Having worked out what I don't want, I now have to work out what I do want. A good way for me to do that is to turn those negative statements into positive ones. Doing it like this makes it easier to be more specific. My list looks like this:

- I want hands to only touch me in a gentle way such as holding hands or stoking my face.
- I want words said to me to be at an appropriate volume, in a gentle, respectful way.
- The only names I want to be called are my actual name, and loving pet names which are special.
- I want freedom to make choices, make mistakes, and make friends without restrictions or rules.
- I want to be encouraged in the things I do, and spoken well of to others.
- I want them to take responsibility for their own actions and decisions, including ones with negative outcomes, and to stand up for me when needed.

- I want them to have a job.
- I want someone who is willing to pitch in, pull their weight, do what is needed.
- I want someone who does what they say they're going to do, keeps their promises and, despite limitations, does what they can do without excuses.
- I want what I need and desire to come before hobbies, sports, organisations or anything else that is not of urgency.

So, now I have a list of expectations for treatment. This list is much more detailed, and outlines clearly what I expect. I am starting to feel my love and respect for me grow just reading it.

For the Reader

Thinking over your life, and the relationships you have had, consider how you have been treated. Make a list of your own of what you don't want in a relationship. Write down everything, even if you feel like you are repeating yourself with some of them. What matters here is that you get it all out and on paper. You need to see it.

Then take those negative statements and turn them into positives. Feel free to use mine if you are stuck and they are appropriate for your statements. It's helpful if you put it into your own words though as they will be easier to remember, and will mean more for you than my words. This part can be quite difficult. It goes against the grain of what we have been brought up with. Take your time. There's no rush.

When you have done that, you are ready for chapter five.

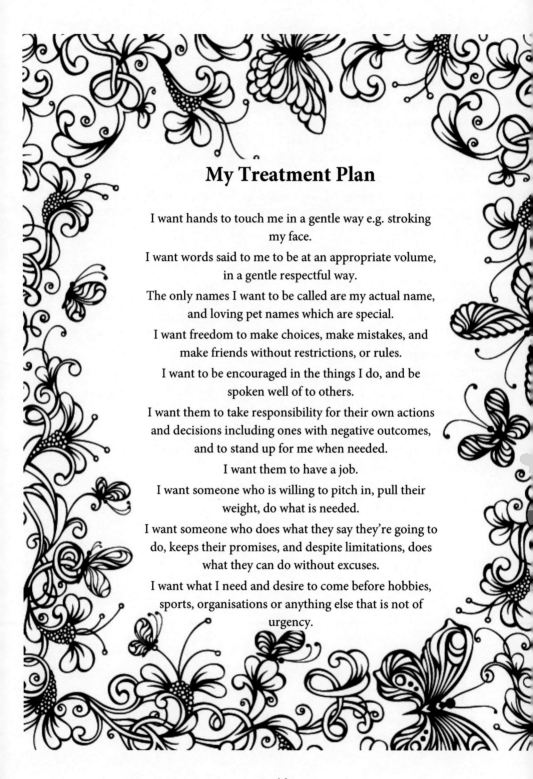

My Treatment Plan

I want hands to touch me in a gentle way e.g. stroking my face.

I want words said to me to be at an appropriate volume, in a gentle respectful way.

The only names I want to be called are my actual name, and loving pet names which are special.

I want freedom to make choices, make mistakes, and make friends without restrictions, or rules.

I want to be encouraged in the things I do, and be spoken well of to others.

I want them to take responsibility for their own actions and decisions including ones with negative outcomes, and to stand up for me when needed.

I want them to have a job.

I want someone who is willing to pitch in, pull their weight, do what is needed.

I want someone who does what they say they're going to do, keeps their promises, and despite limitations, does what they can do without excuses.

I want what I need and desire to come before hobbies, sports, organisations or anything else that is not of urgency.

NOTES

Chapter Five

Impossible = I'm Possible

Do you believe it is possible?

Healing

The sound of wheels churning,
Truth falling into place.
The sound of silent noise swirling,
Lies drifting into space.
Peace entwines itself into shape,
Finds the heart alive.
Grows and breathes the wind around
Until the soul does thrive.

Written by Allison Rose Clark, 01/03/2014

'The only person you are destined to become is the person you decide to be.'

Ralph Waldo Emerson

Believing it is possible and believing in yourself go hand in hand. When I was deciding on the chapter layout of this book, it was difficult to decide which came first. One can't really exist without the other. If you don't believe in yourself, you will also not believe it is possible and hence you will get the result you have always known and thus expect. If you believe things are possible, but do not believe in yourself to achieve them, then the same thing will happen – you will get the result you have always known and thus expect. All the aspects of this "love yourself" thing work together like a fine tuned clock. Each part needs to be working in order for the other parts to do their job. Some parts are so closely related that it is hard to tell where one starts and the other begins.

When I was at school, I used to think how great life would be once school was over for good. No more bullies. No more teasing. I would escape all that abuse. I would finally be free! I believed it was possible – I knew it would happen and looked forward to it with much anticipation!

However, I didn't quite make it to year twelve. I left at the end of year eleven. Most teachers were very surprised. I was top of my classes for Japanese, Italian, and cooking. I always achieved great results. I had a great opportunity at having a bright future. The teachers questioned me as I went about getting signed out but I can't remember what I told them. Rumours went around that I was pregnant. Why was I leaving? The short answer is I panicked. I didn't know it then, but what I had was a panic attack and I left on a whim. In times when a person feels frightened, their response is either fight or flight. It's a survival instinct we all have. For me, I flew away as fast and as far as I could go. I can't even tell you exactly what frightened me in that moment. When I have looked back to try and figure out why, I have felt overwhelmed with fear and doubt. It seemed to be an unclimbable mountain. It appeared impossibly large and there was no way I could conquer it. I had stopped believing that it was possible for me to succeed in life, panicked and left school a year early. I kept telling myself I was going to fail anyway so it didn't matter, in a bid to try and drown out the guilt and shame which followed me afterwards. It was difficult explaining at job interviews why someone with the grades like I had didn't go to year twelve. I can't remember the reasons I spun.

In the years following, I found it harder and harder to believe that good things were possible for me, that I could have a different life, that I could achieve any of my dreams or endeavours, and that courses weren't a waste of my time. Briefly, in no particular order, it looks like this:

- Two office courses – excellent results, no job
- Home based childcare course – excellent results, no job
- Domestic in the healthcare industry course – excellent results, developed dermatitis, no job
- Enrolled nurse – excellent results, two jobs, severe dermatitis so could not continue
- Beauty course – distinction and high distinction, no job
- Mary Kay cosmetics – princess of sales in first year, tried to break out of circle of family and friends in various ways but had too many party orders cancelled and ended up owing five hundred dollars

- Tupperware – did really well in the beginning and started training as a manager, but again, breaking out of the circle of family and friends, despite effort, did not happen

Everything seemed to work against me. This, coupled with all the abuse over the years, took its toll. I totally stopped believing good things were possible for me. I stopped believing that my life would be abuse-free. Being out of the poor house was nothing but a pipe dream. Everything, it seemed, was impossible. It was never going to happen for me. People like me never experience a "rags to riches" type of story. It was just wishful thinking.

Everyone can list all the bad things which have happened to them. Here's a short list of mine:

- I was sexually assaulted when I was eight by my cousin
- My grandfather tried to kiss me with his tongue when I was about twelve
- I was bullied from 1981 to 1991
- My friends betrayed me twice
- My friends deserted me many times
- I was harassed by two thirds of the school population for something I hadn't done
- My boyfriends were jerks
- I have had three abusive marriages
- I have had three miscarriages
- I have mental health issues
- I have allergies which means a lot of products don't agree with my skin
- When I was sixteen my family was nearly wiped out by a truck
- My first serious relationship nearly cost me my life
- I have been abused in every which way you can imagine
- I have been blamed time and time again for things which have gone wrong
- The majority of the courses I have undertaken have not led to work
- Severe dermatitis prevented me continuing with nursing
- My best friend played my youngest sister and I against each other for a number of years
- Every nice thing I ever owned was either damaged, stolen or destroyed by others
- My house was broken into when the twins were about one
- My car was broken into while it was in the back yard in 2004

- I lived with German cockroaches for four years and the twins and I got sick all the time
- I lost my purse with five hundred and seventy dollars in it, the purse being returned three days later with three dollars and my cards in it – my licence and key card, and the purse were all wrecked

That's not a complete list, of course, but you get the picture. All of that, and more, has been constant with virtually no breaks between any of them for thirty-two years. No wonder I am exhausted!

By the time I was forty, I always expected bad things to happen. If something good did happen, it didn't feel real. It must be a trick. If someone was nice to me, it felt fake. I didn't trust them. If I made a new friend, I was always waiting for them to betray me or start hating me. It was always just a matter of time. If someone told me something positive about myself, or made a promise, I didn't believe them. No one was honest with me. If someone asked me to go out with them some place, it felt like a joke. They were not genuine. I did not believe and I stopped trusting that anything good was possible for me. It was always going to be that way.

In the midst of all of this, there has been a higher power looking out for me. You can call it what you like, but for me, I know it is God. There is no way that I could have survived these last thirty-two years without a guardian angel watching over me. Knowing I am not alone gives me strength. It gives me courage to keep on going. It is through His prompting that I have woken up to things earlier than some in similar situations, and have been able to leave despite my fears. It was Him who made me realise I didn't love myself. It's because of these things that I am determined to implement "Operation Love Myself" strictly, no compromising, and no backing down. Whatever your faith is, it is a source of strength for you, so use it to build you up, to give you a safe place, courage and a determination of "stick-to-it-ability".

I can't just leave myself with a list of negative things from my life. It's not helpful. I have to counter it with positive things, such as:

- I have three handsome young men I am proud to call my sons
- Other than the odd migraine, I am rarely sick
- I am good at writing and poetry
- I can draw pretty decently
- I have fantastic parents who help me at the drop of a hat
- I have awesome sisters who I can always rely on to have my back
- I have many true friends who accept me for who I am

- My church family are wonderful and supportive
- My mental health and medication is now stable according to my psychiatrist
- I can handle situations better than I use to
- I can identify the symptoms of my bipolar and OCD and get on top of it before it gets on top of me
- I have a great employer who is flexible and understanding
- I actually feel happy and alive and free!

When the veil was lifted from my eyes and I was able to see clearly that I did not love myself, I instantly knew I wanted to be different towards myself. Reading my positive list fills me with hope and gives me a different perspective on my life. Good things DO happen to me and are in my life! I have started realising that I am where I am because of my own decisions to stay in the abuse. Believing I could attract better people in my life spurred me on to do something actively about it. After all, just realising it, and believing it, on their own will not achieve much. Action is always required to see something move. A child's little red wagon without its wheels is just a tray.

For the Reader

Most people who believe that nothing is possible, or change is not possible, are like that because of all the bad things they perceive are the only things which happens to them in their life. In reality, that is not true. It only seems that way because they don't love themselves enough to see the good. Only the bad sticks out because it justifies the way they see themselves and gives them evidence to back up the way they feel.

What I would like you to do is write down everything which makes you believe change is not possible. These will be all the bad things you see as always happening, the proof you see for nothing good ever happening for you. This is the easy part.

Next, what I would like you to do is to write down all the good things in your life that DO happen and are in your life. For some people this will be difficult. No matter how small the good thing is, write it down. Include absolutely everything you consider as being good in your life or a good experience or event. List as many as you can.

Now, take that negative list and rip it up into tiny little pieces, declaring out loud that you no longer are holding this in your soul as truth, it is all lies, and that they will no longer drive you.

Then pick up that positive list. Read it out loud. Read it again. Feel the inspiration you are injecting into your whole being. Allow yourself to feel the warmth of your own love towards yourself. Feel the happiness rise from your centre. Imagine it shining from your face like the sun.

Another suggestion you might like to consider is keeping a "positive" journal. This is something I do as well. Instead of keeping a diary of your whole day like a normal journal, use this one to keep record of all the positive things which happen to you, no matter how small. Whenever you find yourself thinking, 'nothing good ever happens to me,' pick up your positive journal and read it. Your positive things could include things you are grateful for as well. Believe me, it is a powerful tool in helping you change your negative thoughts about your life into positive ones, and to reinforce to yourself that just because you think it, does not mean it's the truth.

Can you feel the change? Do you believe it is possible now?

It is no longer impossible, but I'm possible!

You should now be able to move onto chapter six.

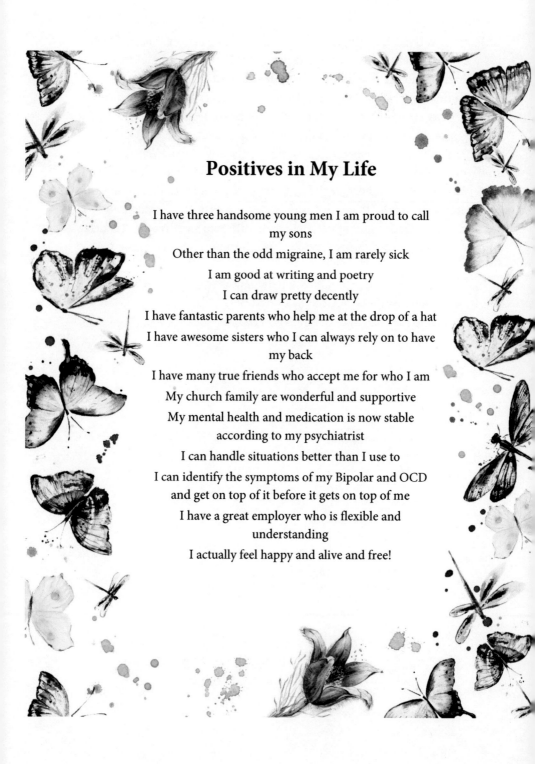

Positives in My Life

I have three handsome young men I am proud to call my sons

Other than the odd migraine, I am rarely sick

I am good at writing and poetry

I can draw pretty decently

I have fantastic parents who help me at the drop of a hat

I have awesome sisters who I can always rely on to have my back

I have many true friends who accept me for who I am

My church family are wonderful and supportive

My mental health and medication is now stable according to my psychiatrist

I can handle situations better than I use to

I can identify the symptoms of my Bipolar and OCD and get on top of it before it gets on top of me

I have a great employer who is flexible and understanding

I actually feel happy and alive and free!

NOTES

Chapter Six

I Think I Can, I Know I Can, I Knew I Could

Do you believe in yourself?

Meant to Be

In the beginning,
Up sprouts a bud,
Offering beauty
Without a word.
Anticipation of
What lies within,
With abated breath,
Waiting with hope.
The petals unravel
In the sun's light.
Dew drops embracing
The dawning of life.

Written by Allison Rose Clark, 27/05/2014

'Whenever you find yourself doubting how far you can go, just remember how far you have come. Remember everything you have faced, all the battles you have won, and all the fears you have overcome.'

Unknown

Always, in the back of my mind, was this little tap, tap, tap, nudge. It was my old pal, Doubt. He has actually been a powerful enemy of my mind for a long time. For me, when I was seven and we moved in 1981 was when Doubt's first talon dug in. It was on my first day at my new school that I first heard the term "four eyes". It was also the first time I had ever been teased for anything at all. At my other school, I was popular, full of confidence, and shy was definitely not a word people would have used to describe me. That talon was to be the beginning of the tearing down of my confidence – the first port of call for Doubt to attack.

I like to picture Doubt to be like a giant hawk. It's not its beauty I picture but its hunting abilities and strength. The hawk hovers, waiting and watching for the perfect moment to swoop down on its prey. With its strong claws, the hawk picks up its prey swiftly. Doubt does the same thing. He is forever watching. When the opportunity arises, he swiftly moves in and clasps his talon around so that you are stuck and can't move. And that is exactly what happens when Doubt strikes – you go nowhere.

'You're no good at anything', 'You're useless', 'You're ugly', 'You're stupid', 'What did you do that for, you idiot?', 'You'll never amount to anything', 'You're a pain', 'You're nothing', 'It was a mistake having you', 'I wish you were dead', 'You're a trouble maker', 'You're nothing but annoying', 'Everything you do is wrong', 'Everything you touch breaks', etc., etc., etc.…

Hearing things like these constantly, over and over again, day in day out, makes you believe it. In my opinion, it is like brainwashing. I wasn't born hating myself. I wasn't even shy when I started school. So, confidence was not something I had lacking. I was assertive – said what I had to say the way I needed to say it. My parents always praised my efforts, so I believed in myself. Through the years of bullying from the time I started school, this changed. Not straight away, but eventually. I did stand up for myself for a while, but it didn't take long for it to break me. My bullies succeeded in brainwashing me into hating myself, putting me outside all truth about the reality of who I was. Building a structure takes time, effort, and commitment. Knocking something down that took years to build can be done in minutes. It takes not much effort at all to complete. Self-esteem, self-worth, and loving yourself can be ruined in just a few words.

Somewhere between my first day at my new school and the end of 1982, my cousin sexually assaulted me. By then, the bullies had been wearing me down with their words. When my cousin asked me to play a game, and I said yes, he asked who wanted to go first. He picked me to be first. The game had to be played in the dark, he said, and when I realised I didn't like this game in the dark I was scared. I screamed until he let me go and ran out into the lounge room. I didn't know what had just happened, but I was very, very scared – petrified! Counsellors have said to me that what I did next showed strength and bravery. Not many eight year olds would think to do it. I went to my mum and said to her that we didn't want our cousin babysitting us anymore. As he was someone we had adored, my mum was confused and asked why, had something happened? I said no, that we liked his sister better as she was more fun. Now, I can't remember if my mum kept on asking questions to make sure or not, but I'm sure she would have, and it doesn't really matter to me. She was not responsible for it, and he never did babysit us again, meaning she had listened to me, possibly suspecting but never entertaining the thought as being truth. We haven't really spoken about it in depth. The fact of the matter, though, is that I was courageous enough to stand up and say something to put a stop to it. I never saw it that way until I heard my counsellor say it. I never had thought about it in terms of the fact that I may not have been physically strong to stop him, but I was still able to stop him. And that is brave!

From that day forward, I withdrew. Before my cousin, a hole had already been started by the bullies. Whatever the bullies said and did to me after that compounded the guilt and worthlessness I had been left with. I became shy, and quite a lot of teachers had to ask me to speak up because I spoke so softly they couldn't hear me. When I was sitting in a room with other people, they would tell me they had forgotten I was there because I was so quiet. I didn't speak unless someone spoke to me. I was fearful all the time.

As I had not realised I had saved us from years of sexual abuse, I always felt guilty that I was not able to protect my sisters. I was to blame for what happened because I had said yes. I thought I had given him permission and so therefore it was my fault. I blamed myself for lots of things after that. I always felt I had to fix things for people, put it right. When I was prefect at my primary school in year six, my youngest sister was always fighting with her best friend. I constantly was helping them to patch up their differences. When they were friends again, I felt I had made something right. When they were not friends, I felt desperate to fix it. Hence, the beginning of me becoming a rescuer.

For the next nine years I would be hounded every day by the bullies. Every day I became more and more convinced they were right. It didn't end at the school gate either. Whenever they saw me out in public, out came the insults and thus-forth. I was targeted at the pool, walking down the street, at the shopping centre, while out the front of my house, at the park, at the skate ramp, and at the library, just to name a few places.

From 1981 until 1991, I attended the Salvation Army Corp for Sunday school. My parents weren't church goers and never forced us to go, but we wanted to go. I made friends with kids there and it was fun. I don't remember in those early days anyone disliking us. The Captain and his wife were people I loved and looked up to. They led that particular corp. for ten years. In that time, they used to call my first sister and I "The Twinnies" because we looked almost identical. I found out years later that they actually thought we were twins! It's funny because we were never in the same aged Sunday school group and don't have the same birthday.

During those Salvation Army days, as the years went on and we got older, new kids our ages started attending. They ignored us a lot. One Sunday, I overheard kids talking about a youth day they had the day before. They had gone skating. I remember feeling disappointed as no one had mentioned it to us or given us the opportunity to go. My parents were poor and the chances of us being able to attend were slim at best, but at least maybe I wouldn't have felt like an outsider who no one liked. I didn't feel like I belonged. The people my own age didn't want to have anything to do with me. I wasn't good enough or cool enough to hang around them. There were many youth days of which not one had been extended to me as being welcome to attend. If you want to make a person feel unwelcome, that's the way to go about it.

One day, the Captain and his wife got transferred to somewhere in Queensland after ten years here. It was a sad day. The Captain and his wife who took over our corp. were lovely, but it was not the same. Things got worse for me. I had decided that I wanted to become a soldier and started the training. During the sessions, questions were asked and I would answer them, but I was often ignored by the leader. I got the message loud and clear I was not wanted there. In the end, my sisters and I hid from the bus one Sunday when they came to pick us up. We didn't have the confidence to just say we weren't going to attend any more. No one came to the door. They never came again. No one ever called to see how these three girls, who had been attending for ten years, and all of a sudden just stop going without a word, were going or why they had left. No one seemed to miss us. It was like we never existed.

In the year I turned fifteen, I joined the first ever netball team at the Police Citizens Youth Club (PCYC) near where I lived. It was the first outside of school sport I had decided to join. Normally I was not the competitive type. But I loved netball at school, and when I heard about this team I wanted to join. I played for two years in the day competition. The first team I was a part of was small. There was only the one team. All the girls were lovely and we were all friends. The second year was two teams. We were left together because we were older than the other girls in the other team. In that team there were girls two years my junior who, unfortunately, were the little sisters of the bullies in my year. Needless to say, they didn't like me from word go. They knew who I was in relation to their sisters.

The coach had her pets – all the bully sisters plus some. She favoured them over any of the others. During training, she would consistently choose these girls when the need arose. After the day comp had finished, most of the girls in my team who also felt the same as me about the coach decided that was their last comp. They weren't coming back next year. I still wanted to play, so signed up for the night comp. The coach had said that training was at five p.m. and so I turned up at the PCYC at 4.50 p.m. When I walked in the door all the other girls were already there. I sat down and they looked at me. One girl said, 'What are you doing here?' I said I had signed up for the night comp and was there for training.

Another girl said, 'Well, training is already over. You're late.' We had a to and fro disagreement about what the coach had said, but they insisted they were telling the truth. I started to feel stupid and left. The next week I turned up at 3.50 p.m. I sat around for an hour. No one turned up. So, as they were making it blatantly clear that they didn't want me playing netball with them, I left the PCYC. I cried all the way home and I never went back.

Such was my life that I expected people to not like me from the moment they met me. The people who accepted me were the other outcasts of the school. The thing we all had in common was that we were bullied by the same people. Some of us copped it more than others though. As the school years progressed, some of my friends were bullied less and less and were eventually accepted by the bullies. However, nothing ever changed for me. My self-worth, self-esteem, and confidence were non-existent. So, when I met Fiancé 1 I didn't notice how he spoke to me or anything because it was probably pretty mild compared to what I had already put up with from school. That was probably the first outward sign that showed that I had already decided that I was worth nothing.

By the time I left school and endured the relationship with Fiancé 1, I didn't believe in myself. I had no confidence at all. I thought of myself as a failure and that nothing would ever work out for me. I would start something, and then doubt my ability to do it and want to quit. Sometimes I followed through. There were a few times where a friend gave me a pep talk and encouraged me to keep on going. She gave me a little card with a poem on it about not quitting. I still have it to this day.

Every time I thought about doing anything I would panic. I didn't believe I could do it. I didn't believe I could handle the responsibility. I didn't believe I would be good at it. I didn't believe that anything good would come from it, so I would be wasting mine and everyone else's time. I didn't believe I could do it on my own, and so on. I did not believe in myself or my abilities. Life was useless and pointless for me.

This has kept up with me until my third marriage was in trouble. During this time, I would be put down even though Hubby 3 didn't think he was. If I cooked dinner and it was different to what we normally ate, he would ask me how I did it. If I said it was a deviation from a recipe, and I used this instead of that, or I just left something out because I had none and no substitute, he would say to me, 'You're not a cook, Allison. Stick to the recipe, that's what it's for.' He did not see that as offensive and rude. He said it was the truth, I should stick to the recipe. I make a nice dinner, which everyone likes, and instead of saying how great it was despite my tweaks, he put it down regardless of it tasting good. In a bid to stick up for myself, I would say that actually I was a cook, a good cook, and reminded him that I had been at the top of my cooking classes at school and knew what I was doing, I'd been doing it for years. Just between you and me, experimenting was what I did in my cooking class at school whenever we had to present a dish of our own. Surprisingly, and interestingly enough, I always got top marks! That means something!

Part of the arguments between Hubby 3 and myself involved me countering some of the things he would say to me, and how he spoke to me. I was beginning to understand this "love yourself" stuff since it dawned on me at our old place. I was becoming more vocal about how he spoke to me and treated me and trying to put in place an expectation. The thing about starting a relationship, allowing mistreatment, and then trying to implement a "new treatment" plan, is that there is going to be backlash. You're no longer predictable. Your behaviour pattern has changed and the same method no longer works on you, and so that can be quite frustrating for them. In some instances, if your partner is able to be honest with themself, things can improve for the better. Action is required, though, not just words. In other instances, if it is about control and power, there will be very little, if any, improvement for the better. Obviously, going into a relationship and having your "treatment plan" in play, the standard is far easier to set. A foundation needs to be strong before anything can be built on it.

Hubby 3 always thought he was listening and could hear anything about himself which was negative because he saw it as a way to improve himself, which was fantastic. The only thing was he never did anything to change the thing he agreed was an issue. Thus, we continued to have arguments about the same stuff. Now, I am not saying I was perfect. I had been living with undiagnosed mental health issues for twenty years or more. I overreacted on some things. I yelled and screamed when I got frustrated. I disassociated from my mind and honestly could not think. I would bash myself in the head and limbs due to being unable to stop the roundabout argument or thoughts in my head. I was not easy to deal with. However, it was also the worst I had ever been. At no other point in my life, or since, had I been that bad. This is going to sound strange, but there is one thing I am grateful for from this third marriage, and that is that without having been with him, my mental health issue would still be undiagnosed and mistreated. If it was not for Hubby 3, I would not be stable today. Essentially, I have him to thank for that.

Having my mum and sister witness a lot of our arguments, and point out the truth to him when they had to, helped me to reinforce in my mind I was not imagining or dreaming things, or making them bigger than they were, and that it was real – this truly was happening in the way it appeared. It helped me to rebuild the confidence I needed to trust my memory and what I knew to be true. It reinforced to me that people believed me and so I was not alone. I was not the only one who could see it. Unfortunately, I also was not the only one to experience some of Hubby 3's traits and attitudes.

One of those people was my youngest. I constantly had to stick up for my youngest. He was constantly being picked on by Hubby 3. The kids didn't realise it but they were treating my youngest the same way as Hubby 3 because Hubby 3 was allowing and encouraging it. He did not see anything wrong with his own behaviour, or the other kids'. It was always the fault of the five or six or seven-year-old boy (the ages he was during my third marriage). Everyone blamed my youngest. I was always accused by everyone that I always took the youngest's side no matter what. If there hadn't been a need for it, I wouldn't have been, but six against one was unfair, and there is no way that ALL the fights were my youngest's fault. One day, when my youngest was six, he said to me at bedtime that he wished he had a different family, that he wished he was someone else, and that no one liked him. My heart broke and wept for him! How can a six year old feel such a way and think such a way? When I tried to reassure him, he didn't accept it as the truth. My little man needed his mum to stick up for him, and so she did! He stuck to me like glue when he was at home, and rarely wanted to stay home if I went anywhere. The day I told him that Hubby 3 was no longer at our house, he was only upset about not seeing Hubby 3's youngest. When we got home he cried. I asked him what was wrong and he said that he couldn't play MineCraft anymore. I realised that Hubby 3 had taken the computer. Ha! So much for having the close bond Hubby 3 thought he had.

Since my third marriage breakdown I have invested into me a lot more love. I have taken the time to take up the things I loved doing but had stopped over the years due to wanting to take on those of my partner. I am listening to music I like and dancing around my lounge room. I am cooking the way I want to. I have discarded my fear of success and taken a chance on a hobby business making cards and unique gifts which I have wanted to do for years. I've stopped watching a lot of TV, sometimes going weeks without watching it, to reduce the amount of negative stuff which is injected into my life on a daily basis. I am finally feeling happy and free! Something which is foreign to me, but with my "treatment" plan, I will not have to feel that way anymore.

For the Reader

Believing in yourself and it is possible is the core of everything. Nothing will change if you cannot believe in yourself or that it is possible. It is the centre wheel of the finely tuned clock which needs to be in working order so it can work at all. Most of the negatives about yourself have already been dealt with in the other chapters. Is there anything from those negatives which you would like to hold onto and keep living with moving forward? If you say yes, ask yourself why. In my opinion, the answer should be there is nothing you would like to hold onto moving forward. But you may think differently. Just so you know, holding onto anything negative will be a pebble in the notch of your new growth. You may not see much, if any, changes or improvements.

Having said that, you need to have some positives about yourself. It was easy to list what you hated about yourself. But what do you like about yourself? This probably will be very hard for some people. It may be the first time you have ever been asked to think of good things about yourself. Let me help you by listing a few positive things about me:

- I am kind
- I like how my hair is slightly wavy when it is short
- I love how I can write good poetry
- I am generous
- I help others when they need it
- I am beautiful

- I have patience with others
- I am outgoing
- I am respectful
- I am friendly
- I have a bright smile
- I am adventurous
- I am worth being loved
- I am valuable
- I am talented
- I love that I have a tattoo
- I am amazing

Now it's your turn. Think of as many positives that you like about yourself as you can. Try to avoid using the word "not" in any of your statements. If you have a "not" statement, try to write it in its opposite. E.g., the statement "I'm not mean", can be turned into "I am kind". It's OK if you can only think of a few to start with. But as you continue with the book, and life in general, when you think of something good about yourself, add it to your list. This list is not one that actually has an end. It is one you can add to indefinitely.

Something you might like to consider is taking your positive lists from chapters five and six, putting them onto a word document, adding some attractive decorations, printing it and laminating it, and then placing it somewhere you will see it every day. Good places are on your bedroom wall or door, on the wardrobe, in the bathroom, on the fridge, at your desk. Place them at your eye level so they are easily noticed when you go to the spot you have put them. You might also like to consider putting them in a frame. When you think negatively about yourself, counter it with a few positives about yourself. We all have been wired wrong that it takes a bit of work to undo the damage. You are not a failure, you are successful. Even if your parents didn't plan you, God did. Take pride in and love yourself. You're allowed to.

So, like the story of "The Little Train Who Could", who said to himself going up the hill, 'I think I can, I know I can, I knew I could,' you know you can too.

You are now ready for chapter seven.

Positives About Me

I am kind

I like how my hair is slightly wavy when it is short

I like how I can write good poetry

I am generous

I help others when they need it

I am beautiful

I have patience with others

I am outgoing

I am respectful

I am friendly

I have a bright smile

I am adventurous

I am worth being loved

I am valuable

I am talented

I love that I have a tattoo

I am amazing

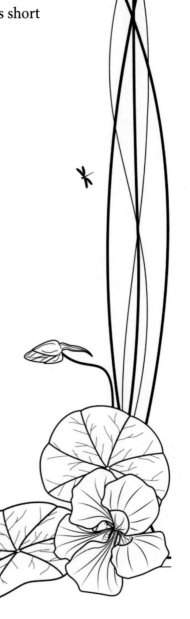

NOTES

Chapter Seven

Stick to Your Guns

Don't compromise

Through All the Turbulations

When I look back on my life
And see where I have been,
It's a wonder how I have survived
The years that I have seen.
Through all the turbulations,
The grief and the abuse,
It would have been really easy
To end it with an excuse,
To say life is not easy,
To say nobody cares,
To say that I've had enough
And that life just isn't fair.
The memories, they are painful.
My heart can take no more.
It's all like a life-long curse
Keeping me burning at the core.
All my feelings churn
And go around and around.
Sometimes I can't help feeling
They're grinding me to the ground.
It goes on unrelenting.
No one knows my inner hell.
I fear it will never end.
I feel I'm locked in a cell.
But I know the fire won't burn for ever
And the pain will one day go.

Memories will give way to peace.
Forgiveness, through my soul, will flow.

Written by Allison Rose Clark, September 2005

'The mighty oak was once a little nut that stood its ground.'

Anonymous

'Never forget: this very moment, we can change our lives. There never was a moment, and never will be, when we are without the power to alter our destiny.'

Steven Pressfield

Ever heard of the phrase, 'hindsight is great'? Well, it is true, hindsight is great. If you don't know what that means, it means that when you look back, you can see what you couldn't before, you can see where you have been. Compromise played a big part all along the way for me. It may not have been a situation where I had a plan which I could see that I was compromising, but I was all the same. I compromised my safety, my life, my children, my mental health, my security, my dreams, my interests, my self-esteem and value, my friendships, and my family – my parents and sisters. I put these men and the abuse ahead of all of that. We all need a healthy balance, which was non-existent for me. I saw that relationship as being more important. What could possibly be more important than loving yourself? Abuse is not love by any definition of the word.

With Fiancé 1, I compromised on absolutely everything. I allowed him to tell me who I could hang around, who my friends could be, where I could go, what time I had to be home hence how long I could be out for, who I could talk to, if I could have my licence, where I could work, if I was able to volunteer my time, if I could attend functions without him with my friends, if I could drink, what I could wear, what our sexual encounters entailed, when I could see my parents and sisters, if I could associate with their partners, what I could do with my hair. He would keep me isolated with no way to contact anyone I knew and left me alone for hours while he gallivanted around the countryside. He had access to my key card and thus all of my money, the way he spoke to me, .etc., etc., etc.

Basically, I was a prisoner and I enabled it by not standing up for myself in the beginning. Even though I am not responsible for the choices he made in how he treated me, I pretty much gave him permission and a green light to go for it because I laid down no ground rules. Guys like this tend to be with women who are timid and easy to control. That's what I was – timid and I didn't have good self-esteem. I was an easy target. My actions became predictable and he knew exactly what to say and do to get me to go back to him. Once I was in that cycle – things OK for a little while; walking on egg shells so not to upset him; cop the abuse; apology and begging; back to being OK for a while; and so it continued – it was hard to break. Each time I did try to speak up for myself, I was met with more abuse, and so it was easier to just accept the apology so it would stop.

He would make threats daily - he would kill me in my sleep; if I ever left him he would beat me up and any guy he might see me with regardless of relationship with that person. I believed him because of all the times he had strangled me and put a pillow over my head. Whenever I saw him come at me with the pillow, I would roll onto my stomach, make a fist with my hand so that there was a pocket of air, and lay there for only God knows how long. I remember thinking this is not the person I fell in love with. He was a stranger and I wanted the other guy back. So, I always thought, maybe this time he will change, he really means it this time. No, I was putting him ahead of my own safety and wellbeing. Abuse is abuse, and I should have left the first day I noticed it. But I didn't. I was not confident enough in myself to do that.

One day, when Fiancé 1 and I lived in the caravan in my parents' back yard, I was looking for my jumper. I asked him for the keys to the car so I could check. He said, 'They're over there,' and pointed towards the microwave. I looked but couldn't see them. I asked where and he said it again. I still couldn't see them, and he got angry, hit me in the arm and said, 'They are here!' He picked them up and threw them at me. Another time, I was doing an assignment for TAFE when he came in to talk to me. I can't remember what about now, but whatever it was I obviously didn't give him the answer he wanted because he dug his elbow into my leg as hard as he could.

I didn't get the strength to stand up for myself and not care about his reaction until he nearly killed me. Every time he wanted sex, I would object because I never felt like I wanted to give it. But he would persist and say that once we got into it, I would want it. Refusing didn't really work, so I would just give in, let him do his business, reluctantly doing whatever he asked me to do, and when it was over, feel like I had been violated. I learnt to hate sex. This time, I didn't want to feel that way. So, I dug my heels in. I was determined not to give in this time. He did his usual thing, but this time I was not reacting the way he wanted. He got angry and threw me on the floor. He pinned my arms down with his legs and said, 'You are going to have fucking sex with me if you fucking want to or not!' I tried to squirm but I couldn't move. I turned my head away while he tried to kiss me and pulled at my night shirt - he was trying to rip it off. Then he put his hands around my neck and squeezed really tightly. I couldn't breathe and was coughing as he pressed against my oesophagus. My face started to feel all tingly and my eye sight started to go all black, and I remember thinking, 'I knew I was going to die this way.' At that precise moment he stopped, got up and left the room. I just lay on the floor trying to get my breath back and recover. Then he walked back in the room and said he wasn't going to give me that satisfaction, and went to our bedroom. I was petrified. I slept in the spare room, if you can call it sleep. All the time I was expecting him to come in and finish off what he had started. Why I didn't just run from the unit I will never really know. I don't understand why I stayed. Why does it take something traumatic to happen before a person wakes up to themself and reality?

This was the biggest compromise I made of all my life. He had to nearly kill me before I got the message that the relationship was toxic and that he didn't really love me.

With Hubby 1, when we disagreed about our future children attending school, with him saying that he wanted to send them to the Catholic school he had attended, I would think, 'We don't have to worry about kids yet. We'll cross that bridge when we come to it.' When he was doing so much for his parents when there were two brothers living at home with them, I would tell myself, 'It doesn't matter.' When his mother wanted to pay for everything when I was pregnant with the twins, he would say, 'Just let her do it. It makes her happy.' And I let her.

With Hubby 2, before we were married, he would only do things with the church if I suggested it, and wouldn't read the Bible unless I read it out loud to him. I would think, 'It'll be different when we are married.' When he would do things for his family at the drop of a hat, and put off plans we had for the day, I would think, 'It will be different when we are married.' When his mum refused to accept the twins as part of our little clan, I would think, 'When we are married, she won't be able to ignore it. It will be different.' But no matter what, it was never different when we got married. In fact, things just got worse.

With Hubby 3, before we got married, we fought all the time. I overlooked it and said, 'It doesn't matter, it is meant to be.' His weight was an issue, and I could see his eating habits weren't crash hot. But I would think, 'When we are married, he will eat better and lose weight, and so it doesn't matter.' His place was always a pig sty – food, dirty dishes and utensils, unwiped benches, rubbish, dirty clothes everywhere, and mould. He would tell me it was depression and that he was not normally like this. I believed him and helped him tidy up. I remember thinking, 'He will be different when he moves from this place and we are married.' When I met him, he was working at a petrol station, cash in hand. All of a sudden, after working there for more than six months (apparently), and only with me for a month, he grew a conscience and left the job. His explanation was that he did not feel right working in that manner, but would get a job the honest way. Hubby 3 got a job working in a rehab facility before we got married, but lost it due to losing his licence from having had too many fines. So, when he said he wanted to work, I believed him, and said to myself, 'It doesn't matter that he doesn't have a job. At least he is looking and wants a job, not like the others. Money is not everything.' In the whole two and a half years we were under the same roof as married, he did not work once, and only looked for work when I was complaining things were tight and we were spending more money than I earned.

Compromising on what appears to be little things, when added together, actually make up a much bigger picture. All the "little" things I compromised ended up growing into a mountain which was unclimbable. One grain of sand in your hand is not very big, but when you keep adding one to it, soon it becomes a pile in your hand. A little makes a lot.

I compromised on how I was being treated, the way I was being spoken to, what I was attracted to, what I could live with and tolerate. Basically, compromising is lying to yourself. When I said all those things to myself, thinking it did not matter, cross the bridge when I come to it, it is meant to be, etc., I was not being honest with myself. I did not stick to my guns. My list, which I showed you in another chapter, though very basic, included "must have a job". I even advised a friend of mine of that particular point once when she was dating. I said to her, 'You don't want to be struggling straight off the bat.' But there I was, having compromised myself on the very same things I had previously advised against. If I hadn't made that compromise, then I may not have married Hubby 3. I had fooled myself into believing a lie. If I can't be honest with myself, who will be?

With the first three relationships, when they started to fall apart, I started to hate them. With Hubby 3, I hated the situation more than I hated him. I felt more on the sorry side for him. Why? Because I had grown up a little, and was willing to admit to my shortcomings. Instead of placing all the responsibility for my happiness and successful marriage on him, I accepted my part in it. I could finally see the truth about myself which contributed to the abuse I let in my life. I did not take on the responsibility of his actions, just my own. No one can control another without their permission.

There is nothing worse than not knowing where to start. In order to stick to my guns, I try to follow this:

- Learn to say "no"
- No matter how nice a person may seem, always speak the truth. They will survive from hearing the truth.
- Don't be afraid to hurt someone's feelings if telling the truth. They will survive that also.
- Say things tactfully, and respectively, wherever possible.
- Even if the truth brings about negative responses, tell it anyway.
- Admit to your mistakes – we all make them.
- Be honest with yourself – no matter how hard.
- Learn when you need help, and ask for it and learn to say "yes" to those who offer.

For the Reader

When you compromise on things, nothing really changes in regards to how you are treated. A cycle is a circle which can become a straight line if we want it to be. Otherwise, you end up where you were at the beginning, time and time again.

Remind yourself of how you want to be treated daily. If you haven't already, put your treatment expectations into a document, laminate it and put it somewhere you will see it. It will help you to determine if someone is mistreating you or not, by your own standards. It will serve you to know them well, so you can lay down the ground rules early on. If they truly care about you, they will respect your expectations. If not, they aren't worthy of your heart.

How would you feel if you received a letter today from yourself? Taking this idea, write a letter from your now self to your past self. What do you want to tell yourself? What wisdom could you pass on to you? You can write it however you like, but this method can be very helpful and healing.

If you don't feel comfortable with the methods I have mentioned, other options or ideas you could consider are:

- Make a poster
- Paint
- Draw

There are no limitations, rights or wrongs. Any idea you come up with will help to remind you of your treatment expectations. It can only be a positive thing.

How's your confidence feeling now? Feeling empowered? Now stick to your guns, don't give up or in.

You should now be ready for chapter eight.

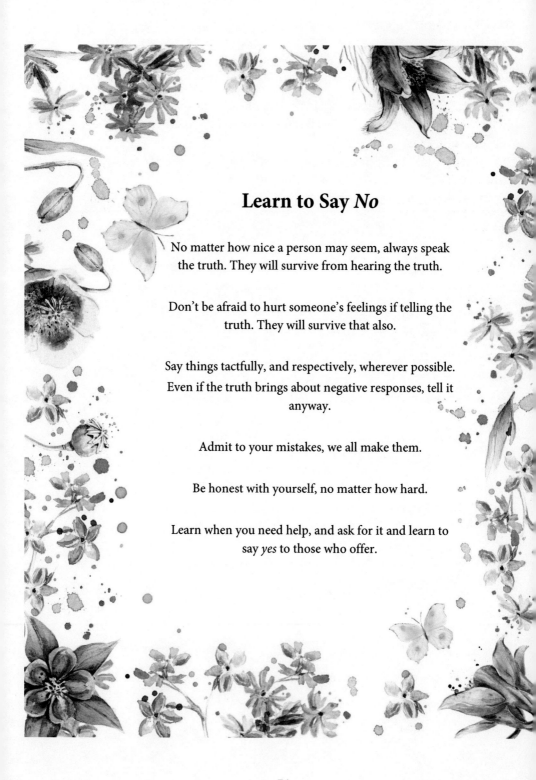

Learn to Say *No*

No matter how nice a person may seem, always speak the truth. They will survive from hearing the truth.

Don't be afraid to hurt someone's feelings if telling the truth. They will survive that also.

Say things tactfully, and respectively, wherever possible. Even if the truth brings about negative responses, tell it anyway.

Admit to your mistakes, we all make them.

Be honest with yourself, no matter how hard.

Learn when you need help, and ask for it and learn to say *yes* to those who offer.

NOTES

Chapter Eight

Silence Is Not Golden

Speak up

Where I Am

Where I am sitting,
It is dark.
It is cold.
I am sitting in
The eye of a tornado.

It is peaceful here.
It is still.
It is silent.
But my thoughts
They entertain me.

Comfort keeps me grounded.
I close my eyes.
Safety is felt.
Danger masquerades itself
As happiness and truth.

Chaos surrounds me.
It is angry.
It is sad.
Raw emotions manifest
Until my body hurts.

Break out from here is risky.
Heart is pounding.
Panic creeps in.
Determination takes over me.
Rising up, I leap into the wind.

Written by Allison Rose Clark, 31/05/2014

'There is no passion to be found playing small – in settling for a life that is less than the one you are capable of living.'

Nelson Mandela

'Never be bullied into silence. Never allow yourself to be made a victim. Accept no one's definition for your life, but define yourself.'

Tim Fields

One thing I was good at was staying quiet. Stay small and say nothing and no one will know I am there. No one could hurt me if they weren't aware of me. I could slip in and out without anyone hearing me or noticing. It was a talent I inherited after being abused by my cousin. My confidence had taken a one way ticket to somewhere else and it didn't look like it was coming back any time soon. I had withdrawn into myself, become very shy, and would hardly talk loud enough for people to hear me.

As I got older, I boasted to people about how I could feel something and no one would be able to tell by looking at me. For example, I could have a migraine which felt like my brain had shrunk and was being bashed against the inside of my skull every time I moved, but I wouldn't dare show it or say anything. If I had a crush on a guy, I wouldn't dare show it or say anything. Not just because of the possibility of being teased, but because I was scared. I was scared of everything. I had no connection between my body and my mind. That, I now realise, was not really a good thing. It's part of disassociation, where your emotions are detached from the rest of you.

All of this was part of the survival techniques I had developed in order to deal with the trauma of my cousin's actions. I always thought if this is how two incidents affect a child, I can't imagine how I would be if it had gone on for years. It had the potential if I had not gone to my mum, but thank God it didn't. I was lucky. These survival techniques were my security. I felt in control and protected. Obviously, that was false security.

I remember once, at the end of year six in primary school, a few of our friends were leaving to start high school at private schools. It was sad, but

I could not cry. Though I was not happy about the situation, there was no lump in the throat, and no welling of tears of the eyes. I was accused of not caring by some of my friends. That's when I was able to put on the waterworks – because someone had hurt my feelings. But it made my friends feel better about how I viewed the tragedy that we wouldn't see these people again. To them, tears equalled sadness. For me, I struggled to understand myself and why I hadn't been able to cry. Did I really not care?

When I was bullied at school, I would tell my mum and she would say, 'Just ignore them.' The usual advice back then, and sometimes these days, but it really wasn't helpful. It was hard to ignore two thirds of your class pea shooting you in the head, or throwing wads of paper at you, or someone stealing your school bag to put it in the bin, or someone shoulder barging you into the railing of the balcony and having to struggle to keep balance to stop from going over. So I stopped telling my mum. There wasn't any point when there was nothing I could actually do. My dad would tell me to punch them, but I didn't have the confidence to do that. So, inevitably, it continued from most of my bullies until I left school.

With Fiancé 1, I stayed quiet. I told no one what was really going on. It was all happy times, rainbows and sunshine when we were in public. But behind closed doors, or when people weren't looking, it was different. I did try to tell a couple of people. The first time was one of Fiancé 1's friends, but I was interrupted by Fiancé 1 before I could really give any details to him. The second time was Mum, when he was living in the caravan with me, but I was again interrupted by Fiancé 1 coming into the kitchen so I didn't really get to tell her much. Every other time I had an opportunity, I was too scared. It was also pride stopping me from being honest with myself, because I didn't want to believe he was as bad as people had told me. I lost my virginity to this guy, and so to me it had to be a forever thing. Our engagement cemented that in my mind. This mentality trapped me in the relationship for much longer than I should have ever let it.

From the very first day at primary school in 1981, to my cousin and the bullying, I had been conditioned to be quiet, put up with everything regardless of how I felt about it, say nothing and tell no one. I did exactly that with everything including Fiancé 1. I put up with anything and everything he dished out on me. I pretended to others and myself that he was a great bloke. I pushed down my hatred of doing sexual things I didn't want to do. I tried to pretend that I liked watching porno videos. I would tell myself that his family were great, even though his sisters hated me for no real reason.

Throughout school I had a couple of instances where I did stand up for myself. Once was during the time I was being shoulder barged and had elbows thrust into my ribcage while walking between classes, mostly. Just after the time I nearly went over the balcony I was standing in the canteen line, when these two girls in my year walked through the line to go to the other side of the quadrangle. It just so happened that they walked through in front of me. The first girl pushed me out of the line, and the other one shoulder barged me and I fell to the ground. I'd had enough. So I got up and ran at the second girl and pushed her. I was ready for a fight. She got the shock of her life because Allison never fought back. The look on her face was priceless as she scurried up and away as fast as she could go. I had to go to the end of the line, but I stood up for myself and so it was worth it. Those two girls never bothered me again.

Another time, I was in year ten and I was walking along a corridor. Someone yelled at me from the balcony above. I looked up and saw a girl from my year with a few of her friends. They said something which was meant to be offensive, but I can't remember what. I remember my reaction though. I said, 'Shut up, you stupid dog.'

Well, all toughness appeared on her scrawny little face and she yelled, 'Say that again, and you're dead at lunch time!' So I did the only thing I could do - I said it again. She threatened that she would knock me out at lunch time, and I told her she knew where I sat. At lunch time I arrived at the usual meeting place to wait for my friends to turn up – at the bottom of the library steps. As I saw her and her friends approach me, I stood up. I was ready to fight, win or lose. She stood about a centimetre from my nose and demanded, 'Now say it to my face!'

So I did –'Shut up, you stupid dog.' She immediately pushed me and I fell backwards onto the steps. I quickly got up and pushed her so hard she fell over onto her butt. She just sat there shellshocked. When it dawned on her that she would actually have to fight rather than just be a bully with just words and no action, she took off. Her friends didn't let her live it down.

I often heard them as they passed me in the corridors. 'Ha ha, you got beat by Allison.' She refused to admit it, but she had walked away – that's defeat! Needless to say, this girl never bothered me again.

I started to stand up for myself and not stay quiet about things more with all the hubbies. I didn't quite get the balance right, but I tried all the same. I wasn't aware of it back then, but I had bipolar II, not depression. I was treated for depression, but the medication never seemed to work because my moods were still all over the place and it never stopped the depression. I would get really, really angry and would feel so overwhelmed by my emotions that I would hit myself in the head and limbs to try and make it all stop. At times I even tried to pull my hair out. There were times following the split from Hubby 2 that I would feel so emotionally overwhelmed that I wanted to cut my heart out and would bash myself in the chest repeatedly. I couldn't deal with it. None of these things I did to myself were ever done lightly – I full on bashed myself up. I even gave myself bruises. That, my friends, is the toll of never allowing myself to feel.

During my marriage to Hubby 2, I developed the ability to escape from what my mind was thinking. I don't recall ever doing it before then. I remember sitting out the front of our home some nights just staring out into yonder, not focused on anything, just staring, and any thoughts that were there I pushed away before I could know what they were. It's true, you can't actually stop thinking until you're dead. Even when you are asleep, your brain is still working. Instead of hearing your own thoughts, they may come to you in a dream. So in the true sense I was still thinking, but I could only feel their presence, not hear their content. I disassociated myself from them. It's quite a difficult thing to do, but now that I do it, I don't know how to stop it. Extreme overwhelming stress is what started it, and so stress is what triggers it.

During my marriage to Hubby 3, this ability to shut my mind down was constantly triggered by our arguments. It was an extremely stressful marriage. I was not able to deal with the stress and this is the only survival technique I had, obviously, that enabled me to escape it. Well, not in reality. I was still bodily present in the room, but my mind refused to be. I was unable to tell anyone what I was thinking because I honestly didn't know. The ability to tap into it while extremely stressed was something I was unable to do.

Now, you may be wondering what that has to do with speaking up. Well, everything, actually. All of my survival techniques have prevented me from making a noise. I lost my voice with them. They made me shy and scared. I had no confidence. They encouraged me to put up with things no matter what. They silenced me. They took away my right to feel safe, loved and cared for. I had no security, no solid ground on which to stand. So I fell, tripped, stumbled, and rolled. When I have tried to speak up for myself, I have done it all wrong. I didn't know how to walk away. I really didn't know what it was I was supposed to be watching out for while dating. In hindsight I could see, but in the present I couldn't.

When it came to my faith, I thought I was listening to God and His guidance. In reality, I wasn't. I compromised all the time, and made excuses and gave explanations for those compromises. I overlooked the things which were pointed out to me. I got what I wanted – the man, no matter what the cost. And pay I did. As I look back, I can see the little things which were pointed out – e.g. the interfering mother of Hubby 1, the interfering mother and sister of Hubby 2, and the size and arguments of Hubby 3, just to name a few. I can also see the times I should have said no and walked away. I can blame God all I want for where I am, but that is just passing the buck and remaining a victim. No, God did not put me in these situations, I did with my choices. God won't take away a person's free will no matter what, good or bad. I failed to speak up for myself. I allowed it to continue even when I knew it was wrong, and it didn't stop. How I tried to tackle it was with anger. Not helpful. Anger just makes an angry person more angry. Anger is not necessarily wrong, but when we start allowing it to determine our actions then it is a problem.

While anger was my main way of dealing with things, by the time I had got to Hubby 3 I was refining my ability to stand up for myself. It wasn't perfect, but at least I was trying not to be angry or yell as much. During an argument I would start off that way. I would be calm, not yell, not use derogative names or offensive hand signals. But it is hard to stay that way for an hour, let alone four hours, which is how long some went for. Hubby 3 wouldn't let me walk away to calm down.

So how does a person stand up for themself? It is not always an easy task. If used at the beginning of all relationships, it makes the process easier. As things crop up, you can respectfully bring it up as being unacceptable. If they care about you and really respect you, they will change their behaviour. Some people are unaware of the things they do because no one has ever told them. Some take it well, and others don't no matter how you say it. But don't let a person's feelings of rejection or hurt by bringing up an issue make you put up with things you don't like and go against your treatment plan. It won't always be possible, but where it is, say it respectfully. Avoid bringing yourself down to their level as there is no reason for you to be down there with them.

It is definitely trickier if you are in a relationship which is abusive already. The severity, and support group e.g. sisters, brothers etc., determines how easy it will be to escape it or change the relationship. You may need outside help and a plan of action. As I am not a counsellor, can welfare worker, or anything else of the sort, I am not qualified to advise on what to do. In one of the following chapters, I will list places where help can be sought which may assist. In the meantime the only person who can stop you from loving you is you.

When abuse is all you have known, it is easy to fall back into that. If you have an idea of what you don't want, and have put it in your treatment plan as the positive opposite, then you have an idea of what you want to look out for. When someone is treating you contrary to that, it is time to speak up. Silence is not really as golden as we are led to believe. It is when it is quiet that trouble is often found.

For the Reader

In order to be able to start standing up for yourself, you really need to know your treatment plan inside out. Not speaking up allows the mistreatment to continue and eats away at how much you love yourself. Any progress you have made will be undone and will reinforce the old ways of thinking and feeling towards yourself.

Practise standing up for yourself. Some role play with someone you trust such as a sister, brother, or best friend may be helpful if you are not confident in how to say what you need to say when it comes to the crunch. You will probably feel stupid at first but like any role play, it gets less awkward with time.

If there are classes in your area which aim at helping you feel confident within yourself, e.g. self-defence, support groups, etc., then can I suggest you look into them? You might like to consider an anger management class if anger is a big issue for you.

If you are a quiet person, or have never had a need to be loud before, you may like to exercise your voice. This is going to sound silly but practice screaming, yelling or speaking very loudly. You would be surprised how many people do not feel comfortable doing any of that. However, if you know you can achieve a loud noise, then you will be confident in using your voice if ever you have to.

One thing you could do if nothing else is write yourself a pep-talk. There will be hard times where sticking up for yourself will feel like it is more trouble than it is worth so you will need some encouragement, especially when there is no one else around to help you in that moment. Write to yourself an encouraging letter which is aimed at helping you to continue with sticking up for yourself.

So shout, be loud, and break the silence. There's nothing golden about it.

Now you are ready for chapter nine.

NOTES

Chapter Nine

Accept No Excuses

Commit to it

Keep Smiling ☺

Even when things
Are going bad,
And people, at you,
Are really mad,
Keep smiling!
Keep smiling!
Even when things aren't
Going your way,
A smile from someone
Can brighten your day.
Keep smiling!
Keep smiling!

Written by Allison Rose Clark, 1995

'There's a difference between interest and commitment. When you are interested in doing something, you do it only when it is convenient. When you're committed to something, you accept no excuses, only results.'

Kenneth Blanchard

The longest and most important relationship you will ever have is with yourself. If you can't love yourself, how can anyone else? After all, you have to live with you twenty-four seven. If you can't even like the person in the mirror, no one else will either. So it is really important that you show yourself the love you have always wanted. It is true that we attract what we illuminate.

In order for anything to really shift in my life, I had to be committed. When it came to having true commitment when I was younger, I didn't have a lot. I didn't persevere through any of the negatives that people would throw at me. I let them defeat me instead. It was always safer to play non-competitive sport as I didn't really have to apply myself too strenuously or seriously. It was easy to walk away from something with the excuse nobody liked me. I left school at the end of year eleven because I panicked and let it overwhelm me which saw me flee instead of sticking it out. I started a desktop publishing course but didn't complete it because I, again, panicked and instead of seeing it to the end I just stopped going and, undoubtedly, I failed. I did this course, and that course, and dibbled and dabbled in training in a number of different industries because, when I didn't get a job from it, I changed direction and interest instead of persevering in the training I had started in order to add to it. I was not committed enough to see that there could possibly be more that I could do to break into that career, and so looked elsewhere. I said I wanted a career, but when it came to committing myself to the process of getting there, my fears were stronger and held me down in a head lock.

When I was about fourteen, my nan and I were driving to a very well-known and popular shopping mall about an hour drive away when she made me promise her that if any guy hit me that I would leave. I didn't keep that promise. I let Fiancé 1 do more than just that to me. I stayed even though he did more than that to me. Even when during a couple of our last break ups I could verbally admit he was abusing me, I still would take him back. When I declared that it was over for good for the umpteenth time, I didn't stick to it. I hadn't committed to the promise I made and let my nan and myself down. All I did was make excuses and make him more important than myself.

One of the few things I was committed to in my life, though, were my marriages. I did everything I could think of to save them, but when only one of you sees the issue you have it is difficult. You can lead a horse to water but you can't make them drink. In the end I walked away knowing that I had done all I could do. Some people tell me I stayed too long and gave too many chances, and for a long time I believed that. These days, I think I wanted to believe in the "us", and tried until I could bear it no longer. A person can only take so much strain before they collapse under it.

During my marriages I attempted different things – Mary Kay, Tupperware, mobile make-up business, making cards and unique gifts. I always had an idea and I would go in determined for it to work, but that is different to being committed to it working. Determination can exist without commitment, which is why I saw a lot of my endeavours fail. I was determined to do something, but not committed enough to last through the tough parts. In my opinion, determination without passion is merely an interest. With passion and a plan it becomes a commitment.

So why was I committed when it came to my marriages, and pretty much nothing else? I think it's because my marriages were important to me, but the other things weren't. When it comes to loving myself, why have I thought that I was not important? I always made excuses for the man, and for me. I need to be as committed to loving me as I was to saving my marriages. Only with loving myself I have to be more so because I can't walk away from me. I can't divorce myself. I can't live under a different roof to myself, or sleep in a different bed. No more excuses! I either become committed to loving myself, or I continue to be committed to hating myself. One will lead me to life, the other to death. I choose to live!

Staying committed, I believe, is the hardest part of all of this. When I started trying to change the way my mind worked, I would get so tired and drained from all the energy I would use in staying positive. It was not unlike swimming ten or more laps of an Olympic swimming pool. The good thing is that over a period of time, not overnight, it got easier. Now, I tend to think positively for the most part. To say it was one hundred percent would be a lie. If I stay committed to my treatment plan with passion and determination as I had been with thinking positive, and accept no excuses from myself, there is no reason why I can't love myself fully.

For the Reader

One way to cement something in is to make a vow, a promise, a pledge. This is different to just making a verbal promise to yourself which you will forget when you walk out the door, such as, 'I swear I am never going to let that happen to me ever again!' This one is going to be written down to remind you as often as you need to, and in many cases that may be daily. You could think of it as a contract if that helps. Be as creative as you want with how you write it down. No one has to see it if you don't want them to. This is being done for your benefit only. Even if you are not creative, a word document can provide you with all the tools you need to make it look great. I believe loving yourself includes taking the time to make the new direction and plan for your future to look fantastic. Who wants to read a drab, plain piece of paper? It's hardly inspiring. Wouldn't you rather look at an awesome picture you created which outlines on it what you value and expect for yourself?

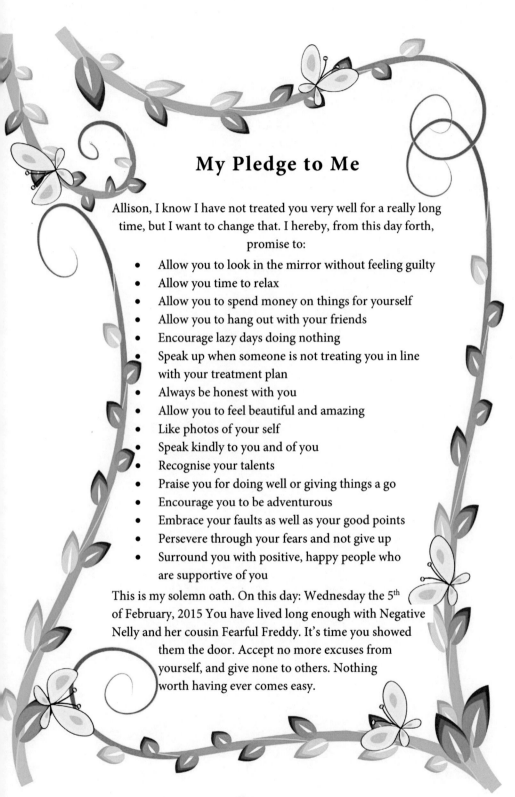

My Pledge to Me

Allison, I know I have not treated you very well for a really long time, but I want to change that. I hereby, from this day forth, promise to:

- Allow you to look in the mirror without feeling guilty
- Allow you time to relax
- Allow you to spend money on things for yourself
- Allow you to hang out with your friends
- Encourage lazy days doing nothing
- Speak up when someone is not treating you in line with your treatment plan
- Always be honest with you
- Allow you to feel beautiful and amazing
- Like photos of your self
- Speak kindly to you and of you
- Recognise your talents
- Praise you for doing well or giving things a go
- Encourage you to be adventurous
- Embrace your faults as well as your good points
- Persevere through your fears and not give up
- Surround you with positive, happy people who are supportive of you

This is my solemn oath. On this day: Wednesday the 5th of February, 2015 You have lived long enough with Negative Nelly and her cousin Fearful Freddy. It's time you showed them the door. Accept no more excuses from yourself, and give none to others. Nothing worth having ever comes easy.

NOTES

Chapter Ten

You Are the Director

Make it happen

Happiness

Be as bright as the sun.
Be as beautiful as a flower.
Be as cheerful as a bird.
Be as accepting as a child.
Have a song in your voice.
Have love in your heart.
Have a spring in your step.
Have stars in your eyes.
Open your eyes and you will see.
Open your heart and you will feel.
Open your mind and you will know.
Open your soul and He will touch you.
Happiness is within you,
Not around you.

Written by Allison Rose Clark: 08/03/2001

'Self-love is an ocean and your heart is a vessel. Make it full, and any excess will spill over into the lives of the people you hold dear. But you must come first.'

Beau Taplin

Up until now I have allowed myself to be controlled by others. It's always been about their interests and their hobbies, their desires, their choices, their dreams. I have allowed them to be the rudder of my boat, steering me where they want to go. Their hobbies, interests, friends and dreams became mine. I had none of my own. There were no favourite foods, books or movies. Everything about me reflected that of my partner. As soon as that relationship was over my interest in any of their things just vanished in a cloud of smoke. Instantly gone. My likes and dislikes were as stable as my relationships.

Unsurprisingly, at the end of each relationship I felt like I didn't know who I was. And it was true! For the most part anyway. Just as I would be getting to know me, someone would come along and I'd let myself get absorbed into who they were. Then bam! Back to square one.

Though temporarily on holiday, there were some things I knew about myself. Such as that I love to write poetry and short stories. That has never dwindled my whole life. It's the only thing that never slipped away from me. I also like to draw and do crafty things. I'm creative. All these things went a little quiet for a few years, but they were still there, like a seed covered in snow. When the spring time comes, the snow melts and the seed grows. That's how I imagine my talents - hidden under the snow from the storm that's been my life. Now the spring has arrived, my newfound self-love and respect seed has started to sprout and grow in the sunlight of a new beginning.

All this shows me that I had relinquished the control of my life to another person. Essentially, the person I was with them as opposed to the person I should have been. My life lacked direction. I wanted things to be different, but unknowingly at the time, I was doing everything the same, relationship in and relationship out.

When marriage number three ended, I'd hit rock bottom on every single level – heart, mind, body, soul and spiritually. I had to start being brutally honest with myself. If not then I was doomed to remain where I was. There was no future without change. No change without choice. No choice without direction. No direction without a purpose. Instead of letting others direct my life, I had to take the reins and learn how to be my own director. My life is the stage, I decide who the leading lady is, and I decide where the story goes. I decide how the leading lady behaves and thinks. The leading lady – she is me! So I need to be me.

One thing I have always had trouble with is putting myself first. It isn't exclusively a woman thing. A lot of people put others ahead of themselves, much of the time to their detriment. I have found that in order for myself to be able to do this effectively, I have had to learn how to say the dreaded word "no", and know when to ask for, and accept, help from others. I have also had to make some really tough decisions which have broken my heart.

When I was younger, whatever someone asked for or needed, I would say, "yes" or "I can help". That on its own is not really an issue. It's right to help people when they need it. However, it does start to be an issue if you can't say "no" when you need to, or you become over committed. I always felt like I was letting someone down if I said no, and that made me feel guilty because it felt like I was saying they weren't important. In reality that's false, but it's amazing the things your brain will spin and you will believe just because your head told you so. Not every thought you have is the truth. For example, it isn't truth when your head tells you that you are ugly, or you have no friends, or that you are worthless. So, when you need to say no, and your head tells you that you are being mean, uncaring and selfish, then it isn't being honest with you. Remind yourself of the facts for your decision so that thought can be put in its place. And that place is in the garbage with last night's leftovers!

As a people pleaser, saying yes was natural. Saying no wasn't. I felt uncomfortable, like I was walking barefoot over pebbles. However, being unable to say no was effectively making others more important than myself, and thus any of my needs were nothing in comparison and therefore could always wait. Effectively, they were in control, directing my time and, overall, my life. The truth is, no matter who you are, not every single time someone needs help is a dire strait life and death situation. It is OK in times of non-urgent requests to consider yourself and your commitments before you agree to help.

Learning to say "no" is another very important step in loving yourself correctly. Courage and determination are also important. You will need them all to successfully transition from your old ways to your new ways.

It wasn't until recently, with the help of my psychologist, that I have come to realise that I have more courage and determination in me than I ever knew was there. I certainly have not felt courageous! I have always felt shy, reserved, scared, unworthy, unlikable, and cursed. I don't recall any other time of bravery and courage prior, so the first time in my memory where I displayed this courage and determination was after my cousin sexually assaulted me. My psychologist told me I should feel proud that I had the courage to stand against my cousin and approach my mum the way I did, and that I was determined to see it not happen again. She told me that it was clever of me. I guess there are other extenuating circumstances that made it a little easier, such as that I didn't live in the same house as him, but by no means was it an easy thing to do. The fact remains, however, that

I was eight and scared and that was the only approach I had in order to try to stop it. I took control, and it worked!

For the Reader

Love cannot be found where it isn't living. It can only happen from the inside out. Once you start loving yourself, all the other areas of your life will come together and have a domino effect. People will either respect you or walk away, effectively eliminating the negatives and leaving behind the positives - a bit like sifting clumps out of flour. Don't be surprised if you are feeling tired and drained. It takes a lot of energy. But don't give up. Persevere, because the end reward is so worth it.

At this point, revise your treatment plan, letter to yourself, positive things about yourself, positive things in your life, and your pep talk to yourself. You should be feeling pretty happy and loving yourself more than you did ten chapters ago. There is one more thing you need to do for yourself, and that is to consider in what ways you can show yourself love.

What is it that you like to do? What sort of things help you to relax? What makes you feel beautiful? Do you feel fantastic when you wear a certain lipstick or dress, for instance? Do you receive compliments when you wear a certain outfit or colour? Take a little bit of time to make a list of ways you can show yourself that you can love you.

Here is my list:

- Take a long hot bubble bath while listening to music and enjoying a nice glass of wine.
- Read a book while snug in bed, eating chocolate and drinking wine.
- Watch a movie while in bed, eating chocolate and enjoying a nice glass of my favourite liqueur.
- Take a nice stroll along the beach or along the bike track around the lake.
- Wear my favourite perfume all the time, not just when I go out.
- Wear my shiny shoes whenever I want.
- Wear my sexy underwear all the time, not just when I'm going out.
- Sit out the back on the veranda overlooking the lake, enjoying a cup of coffee and taking in the nature around me.
- Veg out on the lounge while listening to my favourite music.
- Put on my favourite music and dance around the lounge room however I feel like.

- When someone pays me a compliment, say "thank you" without adding an explanation. It's OK to accept it and feel good about it.
- Spend money on myself, not just other people, and it's ok to feel good about it.
- Spend time with my friends.
- Go to the cinemas.
- Drink at a coffee shop
- Eat ice cream from cold rock or the ice creamery.

Now, stand up straight and walk tall. Are you ready to be the director? The stage awaits.

NOTES

Chapter Eleven

Find a Rock to Stand On

Finding help and support.

Standing on a Rock

The waves are lapping
At my ankles.
The wind is strong
Against my body.
The sun is harsh
Upon my face.
The sand is fiercely
Blasting my skin.
The tide is quickly rising.
The sun is setting in hues of red.
But as I stand upon this rock
There's no way that I am moving.
It is resilient and firm.
It is unshakable ground.
An earthquake vibrates
But still I stand.
Then someone pushes
And another pulls.
They are firing arrows
But still I stand.

Written by Allison Rose Clark, 18/3/2015

'There are times when we have to step into the darkness in faith, confident that God will place solid ground beneath our feet once we do.'

Dieter F. Uchtdorf

'Whether you think you can, or think you can't, you're right.'

Henry Ford

A house is no good without a solid floor, strong supports, or a stable ground to build it on. Without these the house will not stand the test of time. The weather will wear it down if its foundations are weak. It is no different when it comes to loving yourself. The roof is your treatment plan and direction, the walls and beams are your support systems and other activities which aid in upholding them, and the floor is your belief system which helps to give all these strength to keep on standing through the storms.

So it's important to believe in something. It is well known that having faith in something higher than ourselves helps us to cope through the tough times.

For me that belief is in Christianity, in Jesus Christ. I believe that Jesus Christ was sent to earth by God in order to give us a chance at something better than what this life can offer us.

'For God so loved the world that he sent his one and only son that whoever should believe in him shall not perish but have eternal life.'

John 3:16.

God calls this second chance eternal life. I call it spiritual CPR.

Now you may not believe in God or Jesus, but still believe that there's something out there greater than ourselves. Whatever it is that you believe in, make sure that you are firm in it. It needs to be able to give you strength and courage to persevere through the tough times that will follow you through your life. There will be times where you slip from your treatment plan and will need that solid rock to keep you standing. You're human. No one is perfect so to expect perfection in keeping with your treatment plan is a certain way to make sure you fail.

Jesus gives me strength and courage to face life. Always has. I have got angry at Him and I have screamed at Him and I have asked Him why and I have cried over all the things happening to me. It's OK. He can handle it. God wants me to take to him all of my problems, all of my worries, all of my sadness, all of my anger, absolutely everything and anything which is upsetting me. His shoulders are broad and his burden is light and so He can carry the whole world if need be.

'He lifted me out of the pit of despair, out of the mud and the mire. He set my feet on solid ground and steadied me as I walked along.'

Psalm 40: 2

Without God as my solid rock to stand on, I honestly don't know where I would be today. I can imagine that I may be dead, my very life taken by the hands of somebody who claimed to love me. Fiancé 1 didn't just stop because he got a pang of conscience. He stopped at the precise moment that I thought, 'I knew I was going to die this way.' No one else other than myself and God could have heard what I thought and I don't believe in coincidence. You might like to say that my guardian angel stepped in. I would be inclined to agree with you. Angels are the messengers of God doing His Will on this earth. Obviously, it wasn't my time to meet my maker.

One thing I aim at is not putting my faith in people. People are hypocrites and unreliable when it comes to not hurting me or letting me down. They are human. They are not any more perfect than me. I will inevitably hurt somebody or let them down no matter how unintentional it is. We are all in the same boat and heaven is full of us hypocrites. So it's silly of me to put my faith in somebody or something that doesn't have a higher purpose than humanity. However, you may think differently.

In addition to having a faith, you need a support system. A support system is available help when you need it. It could be a best friend, a relative, or another person who knows what it's like to experience what you're going through. Most of us have someone who is very close to us who we trust and confide everything to. Our support systems may be available to us twenty-four hours, seven days a week, especially if there is more than one person you can turn to. They also may not be. But don't despair. There is help out there which you can access twenty-four hours, seven days a week. At the end of the chapter I will list a few Australian national help lines and websites which I, and others I know, have used.

Sadly, for the majority of us who don't love ourselves, we didn't get there without having experienced some bad things. That means that there could be other issues which have been contributing to your lack of self-love. There's no easy way around it. You have to deal with it. If you don't face it, there's a good chance that you will repeat some mistakes because those past hurts are the reason for your bad choices. Everything interlocks like a zipper. For this reason, you may like to consider some counselling or psychology help (at the end of the book, you will find an explanation outlining their differences). Don't expect too much of yourself though. Some things will be a lifelong journey. Most things will be easier to deal with if you are aware of them. When you can recognise when you are repeating your past decisions and lack of love, you will be able to see where and how you need to take control of it so that you can turn it around.

Lastly, and very importantly, get out. Get out of the house. Get out of your head. Get out with your friends. Get out into the community. Get out to an event. Whatever you do, just get out there and do it. Not only will you feel good for having done something with your day other than go over again with yourself how much life sucks, but you will be making new friends, socialising in a fun and happy way, contributing to society, and creating new habits and routines which will inevitably reinforce how you love yourself and give your life purpose and meaning.

Yep, all this is easier said than done, but nothing good ever happens easily. That's why you need your rock to stand on - a solid sturdy foundation.

For the Reader

Believe it or not, there is help out there, but the hard part is knowing where to start looking. I have listed some of the things I, and others I know, have utilised for ourselves or someone we know. These are specific to Australia, but if your search is for yourself or someone else international, I can't see the harm in taking advantage of some of their online information and tests. There are many good ideas that can be taken from them which will be beneficial to anyone no matter where they are from.

Beyond Blue

www.beyondblue.org.au

Beyond blue is a national initiative to raise awareness of anxiety and depression.

Beyond blue offers:

• Twenty-four hour call line - 1 300 22 46 36

• An online community where a person can talk through any issue through a forum.

• Lots of resources and information.

Youth Beyond Blue

www.youthbeyondblue.com

Youth beyond blue is a service aimed at suicide prevention, depression and anxiety for people up to the age twenty-five. They encourage young people to talk to someone.

Youth beyond blue offers a twenty-four hour helpline - 1300 22 46 36, and an online chat from three p.m. to midnight.

The website offers lots of information on things such as suicide prevention, depression, anxiety, self-harm, alcohol and drugs. Other help on the website includes:

• Do something

• Help someone

• Get involved

All these tabs have drop menus to choose from.

• The brave program

Is an interactive online program for the prevention and treatment of anxiety.

Lifeline

www.lifeline.org.au

Lifeline is a twenty-four hour service in crisis support and suicide prevention.

Lifeline offers:

• Twenty-four hour helpline - 13 11 14

• An online one on one crisis chat operating seven days from seven p.m. to four a.m. (AEST)

• An online directory of free or low cost health and community services Australia-wide

• Facts and information

• Preventing suicide - helpful steps and information

• Self-help tools - information aimed to help yourself manage

Black Dog Institute

www.blackdoginstitute.org.au

Black dog is a not for profit organisation and world leader in diagnosis, treatment and prevention of mood disorders such as depression and bipolar disorders. They are pioneers in the management and treatment of mood disorders. There is much to this website and it will pay to check it out.

Examples of what is available are:

• Self tests - these help to evaluate the likelihood of further investigation.

• Psychiatrists are on site to help diagnose mood disorders and appointments are necessary if you would like to see one after completing the self tests.

- Fact sheets
- Research
- Education

Contact details can be found on the website

Blue Knot Foundation

Formerly ASCA - Adults Surviving Child Abuse

www.blueknot.org.au

Blue Knot Foundation is the leading national organisation working to improve the lives of those who have experienced childhood trauma, including neglect and domestic violence in childhood

Blue Knot help line 1 300 657 380

They offer phone counselling support, information, resources, tools and workshops to survivors and their family and friends.

There are services such as a development training, available for those who work with survivors, across all sectors.

Blue Knot Foundation also offers:

- Fact sheets
- Newsletter
- Videos
- Ways to get involved

* Podcasts

* Links to other services and organisations in each state and territory in Australia

Headspace

www.headspace.org.au

Headspace is the National Youth Mental Health Foundation, which helps young people (up to age twenty-five) who are going through a tough time.

The following offer counselling services among other things:

Salvation Army Australia

www.salvationarmy.org.au

St Vincent de Paul

www.vinnies.org.au

Anglicare

www.anglicare.org.au

Victims of crime

www.victimsofcrime.com.au

Phone - 1800 00 00 55

Head office is in Victoria.

Victims of crime are a private entity which has been assisting victims of crime for over fifteen years.

If you have been a victim of child sexual abuse, you may be entitled to free counselling.

You can fill out an enquiry form or call. You don't need to have reported the crime to the police in order to apply for counselling assistance. The Medicare ten counselling sessions can be used in conjunction.

If you are seeking compensation you will need an incident number.

Victims of crime can assign you a counsellor or psychologist, or you can nominate your own if you have one. If you do have a counsellor you may like to discuss this with them before applying as they may have to be registered as trauma counsellors with the victims of crime in order to nominate them.

Try using Google to find support groups in your area for depression, anxiety, bipolar, etc. I've attended groups for domestic violence, depression including postnatal, anxiety, and child abuse and trauma.

You might like to consider classes which help you to feel good and enhance your skills such as yoga, pilates, meditation, or gym. I've attended classes for meditation and parenting skills over the years.

Do you have a hobby or an interest? Try to Google for them in your area to find groups or workshops. I used to attend card making and writing workshops. If you don't have any interests or hobbies, here are a few other ideas: craft, sport clubs e.g. volleyball or basketball, chess club, car enthusiasts, photography, painting, drawing, knitting, sewing, etc.

I don't know what religion based help is out there for other faiths, however, for Christians there are a few. They are found in the form of healing retreats or centres and prayer meetings and centres. Also, you may like to consider a Christian counsellor or psychologist, though they are harder to locate. Over the years I have found that a few of my therapists just so happened to be Christian. God supplied what I needed. As a Christian, I have also found it helpful to listen to Christian based radio stations. On the South Coast, NSW, I can't speak highly enough of Pulse 94.1FM as they have played a vital role in my life since my first marriage breakdown. If your faith is different to mine, your church leaders, or people you know, may be able to help you to locate some faith-based help and services. Otherwise, there is always Google.

And don't forget your friendly GP, who can refer you to services such as counselling.

Can you see your rock now? Your solid ground? Well, go and stand on it!

NOTES

Chapter Twelve

Out with the Old

Make a new beginning

I Am Happy

Feeling the warmth of a brand new day,
Gives the sense of a new beginning,
That anything is possible.
Fills me with joy and love
And that life is good.
It makes me smile.
And my thoughts are positive in that moment.
I am at peace in my centre.
I am happy!

Written by Allison Rose Clark, 27/10/2014

'Your value doesn't decrease based on someone's inability to see your worth.'

Dr Laura

You are amazing! You are beautiful! You are courageous! You are brave! You are strong! You are incredible! You are wonderful! You are tough! You are a winner! You are a champion! But most of all you are a SURVIVOR!!!

It has taken me fifteen years to find the right counsellor or psychologist. It has taken me twenty years to find the right doctor who would take me seriously. It has taken me about thirty years to discover my mental health issues. And it has taken me thirty-two years to forgive and love me.

I never stopped searching for help. I never gave up. I never stopped looking for answers.

I was born in an era where child sexual abuse was denied, buried, and turned a blind eye to. I was born in an era when mental health issues were either denied, ignored or considered insanity. It was only as I grew up that these sorts of things were being admitted, taken seriously, and exposed. During my childhood, it was only just being acknowledged and admitted that a child hadn't done something to arouse the sexual interest of an adult.

During my whole journey, I have not had anybody give me the direction that I have needed. Nobody ever told me the things that I have discovered. I have felt isolated. I have felt alone. I have felt condemned. I have felt lost. Many times I have felt like a fraud. It's been a long, hard and often bumpy road full of potholes.

I have wasted twenty-four years of my life with four different men who have treated me badly. That's twenty-four years I've lost and I can't get back. I feel cheated out of a life which could have been happy. I've had three failed marriages instead of one successful one. I haven't had the safety, security or love that I have deserved. There are many, many other people out there who currently are wasting their life, who are doing the same things that I have done and allowed to happen to myself. My life story has to help somebody, somewhere, and save them from years of unhappiness and searching for love in all the wrong places. If I can help just one person through this book, then that is one person who will feel happy and loved by the one person that matters the most – themself!

It's now time to make a new beginning. This is the springtime of your life. Time for your seed to sprout from under the snow. That seed is going to grow into the biggest, tallest and strongest tree this world has ever seen! Did you know that the smallest seed is a mustard seed, and that the mustard seed grows into a massive tree, one of the largest? All you need is a little bit of hope and big things can happen.

For the Reader

Congratulations! You have reached the end of the book. You should feel very proud because this loving yourself is a big step. It's a major thing. Everything in our life pretty much pivots on it and we don't even realise it. Now you've been equipped with tools which you can use every day, year in, year out, and it will never go out of fashion or be outdated, and can be used generation after generation. It is valuable, priceless knowledge. Don't leave home without it, ya hear!

How fantastic does it feel to have renewed hope, to know you're worth more than you ever imagined? Enough to jump for joy? Enough to dance and sing? How about enough to put a fire in your belly for a fresh start?

Your new story starts when you turn the first page. Go and rewrite your journey.

What Difference Does It Make?

Psychiatrist

A medical practitioner specialising in the diagnosis and treatment of mental illness.

Clinical psychologist

Specialises in the assessment, diagnosis and treatment of a range of emotional, behavioural and relational issues. They are trained in using structured and specialised therapies which are typically more effective then general supportive counselling.

Psychologist

An expert in human behaviour and emotion, studies mind and behaviour. Their skills can be applied to a variety of fields such as health, education and management. They can also help mentally healthy people in areas such as handling stress and family problems.

Counsellor

A person trained to give guidance with personal psychological issues. They assist people to better understand themselves by explaining options, setting goals, and helping them to take action. They focus on the client's concerns and difficulties, including understanding people's patterns of thoughts, behaviours, feelings and ways the person can better understand themself to make changes in their life.

The Last Say

What we know of this world is that most of the abuse that is suffered is by women at the hands of men. Let us not forget that abuse does happen to men at the hands of women and is under reported. Traditionally, men are seen as the stronger of the pair, and that is true in the majority of relationships, but there are plenty of men who would never lay a hand on a woman no matter what she did to him. So, in the notion of fairness, this book is primarily aimed at women due to myself being a woman. However, abuse is abuse and there is never ever a good excuse for it, and no one anywhere should ever put up with it, no matter what! Ever!

*****

NOTES

111

Demons of My Past

The Fall Is Broken

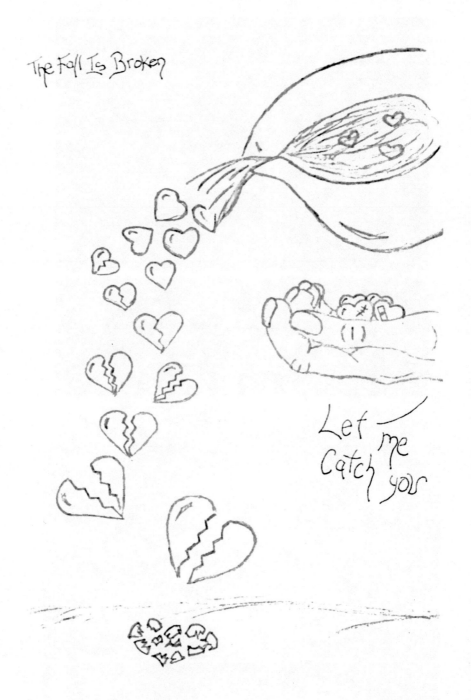

Let me
Catch me
you

The Fall is Broken

Our journey from birth starts off whole, new and unblemished.
Throughout our life, experiences in life crack us and we become broken.
Some break more than others.
Hence, our fall through life is broken.
But our fall can be broken only by God.
He'll break your fall if you ask Him and He will catch you.
He will mend the breaks and make you whole again.
Only this time, there's scars that have a story you can share and inspire others with.
Our fall is broken in life.
Our fall is broken by God.

THE FALL IS BROKEN.

15/10/14

The Ghostly White Forest of Despair

Heart In A Box

Matthew
6:28-29

Matthew 9:28-29

So why do you worry about clothing? Consider the lillies of the field, how they grow; they neither toil nor spin; and yet I say to you that even Solomon in all his glory was not arrayed like one of those.

My Tears Remember

At Pulse 94.1FM studio 2015

Yesterday's Chains

Survived